D1880805

THE BIRDS OF CALCUTTA

Owing to the antiquity and rarity of this book, certain pages are regrettably absent, and readability is compromised due to the blurring of the original text. If you possess any insights regarding the availability of these missing sections, kindly inform us. Your assistance is crucial in ensuring the completion of this significant work for the benefit of future generations.

THE BIRDS OF CALCUTTA

FRANK FINN

GYAN

Published by

Gyan Publishing House
5, Ansari Road
Daryaganj, New Delhi-110002
Phone: 011-47034999, 9811692060
E-mail: books@gyanbooks.com

Distribution Network
gyanbooks.com
India, USA, Canada, UK, Australia

© Publisher

All rights reserved. No part of this work may be reproduced, stored, adapted, or transmitted in any form or by any means, electronic, mechanical, photocopying, micro-filming, recording or otherwise, or translated in any language, without the prior written permission of the copyright owner and the publisher.

ISBN: 978-93-7316-383-3 (HB)

First Published, 1904

2nd Impression 2025

Printed at: Gyan Press, Delhi.

The book is sold subject to the condition that it shall not, by way of trade or otherwise, be lent, resold, hired out, or otherwise circulated without the prior publisher's written consent.

THE BIRDS OF CALCUTTA

Arthur: FRANK FINN

THE
BIRDS OF CALCUTTA.

THE

THE BIRDS OF CALCUTTA

BY

FRANK FINN, B.A. (OXON.), F.Z.S., M.B.O.U.,

AUTHOR OF "FANCY WATER-FOWL," "HOW TO KNOW THE INDIAN DUCKS," "HOW TO KNOW THE INDIAN WADERS," &c.

SECOND EDITION.

Calcutta:

THACKER, SPINK & CO.

1904.

CONTENTS.

PREFACE TO THE SECOND EDITION.

THE kind reception accorded to the first edition of the present little work has been deemed a justification for its reproduction in an improved form. A few necessary alterations have been made to bring it up to date, and the chapters have been re-arranged so as to bring the birds dealt with into the same order as that in which they occur in the *Fauna of British India*, Bird volumes. The scientific names used for Indian birds are those of the above work, the few foreign species mentioned bearing the name given them in the *British Museum Catalogue of Birds*.

The usefulness of the book will, it is hoped, be enhanced by the illustrations, which have been drawn by that well-known ornithological artist, Mr. Herbert Goodchild, in most cases from living birds in the collection of the London Zoological Society.

FRANK FINN.

LONDON, *January* 1904.

THE BIRDS OF CALCUTTA.

I.—THE CROW.

"*Even the blackest of them all, the Crow.*"—*Longfellow.*

BLACK though he is, the Crow may fairly head the list for more reasons than one. His clan is reckoned by most ornithologists as the most blue-blooded among the birds, and comes first in the order of precedence in the official list in the "Fauna of British India." And he himself, full no doubt of consciousness of his egregious merits, has already made his bow to all my readers, even if they have resided in India but for a day. Various people have amused themselves at the expense of naturalists who call him *Corvus splendens*, but it would be hard to find a better name. See him, as I first saw him, in the London Zoo among a number of other species of his kind, and you will at once pronounce him the sleekest, glossiest, and best got-up fellow of the lot, for most of his upper plumage has an exquisite satiny gloss of purple and green, admirably set off by his grey neck and coal-black mask and cap. In this pattern of colour, as well as in size, he certainly very much recalls the jackdaw (*Corvus monedula*) at home, but he has a very much longer and heavier bill, and dark instead of white eyes. The difference between the two species may be at once noticed even in the mounted specimens in a Museum, and is much more conspicuous in the living birds, as specific distinctions most commonly are.

There is nothing to choose in the matter of gloss and richness of plumage between the male and female Crows, but the former's bigger head and bill will distinguish him easily if both are seen together: the difference in feature is hardly marked enough to sex any Crow by itself. Young Crows when they leave the nest have light blue eyes and pink mouths, but they do not look innocent on that account—rather, with their duller, shabbier plumage, more blackguardly than their dark-eyed, black-mawed parents; the old Crow being, if anything, rather blacker inside than out, as far as one can see when he opens his mouth to caw.

The Crow, unlike the Ethiopian of Scripture, can change his skin, or rather his feathers, for pied, white and dun-coloured specimens are not unknown; one of the last mentioned kind lived for more than a dozen years in the Alipore Zoo. The white birds have flesh-coloured legs and beaks, and in the duns the parts that should be grey in the normally-coloured Crow are lighter than the rest. Such "off-coloured" Crows are said to be tabooed by Crow society, but this does not seem to be the case with birds suffering from deformity or disease. I knew for years a Crow residing in or near Sudder Street which suffered from some unsightly and doubtless highly unpleasant disease of the feet, which makes those members look as if the bird had just been walking in thick mud; and evidently they were very tender, judging from the gingerly way in which this sufferer walked. Yet I cannot doubt from the many accounts I have received of it that a damaged Crow is often worried to death by its fellows, and I myself once saw one that seemed to have been having a very bad time at their hands, or what did duty as such. But, nevertheless, the Crow is a bird of many social virtues; he will certainly rescue a friend in distress if he can, for his evident and loudly expressed indignation when one handles a dead or living comrade of his makes it plain that a less powerful enemy than man would probably be seriously attacked. Also he is a good husband, feeding his wife assiduously, and letting her pull their common booty away from him; and a tender parent, much attached to his abominable offspring, in defence of which Crows will attack even a human being at times. The Crow, however, while looking leniently on head-tickling and such-like simple connubial reciprocities, is very severe upon any unfortunate couple of his kind who go too far in a public display of affection, as I have witnessed on more than one occasion; and as for the wing-drooping, tail-cocking strut which the English cook indulges in during the breeding season, any Calcutta Crow who presumed to show off in such a way would most likely be very soon taught that it was "no matter for his swellings, nor his turkey-cocks." This persistent interference by Crows in each other's domestic affairs may be the reason why there seem to be so few nests in proportion to the numbers of Crows one sees. Although this Crow lives so much in the company of man, it has not taken much to nesting in buildings, usually preferring a tree; though here and there pairs will attempt a nest on a house, and Mr. B. Aitken, in Hume's "Nests and Eggs of Indian Birds," has given a long and amusing account of an idiotic couple who wasted a whole breeding season in trying to make nests in utterly impossible positions in the verandah of the *Madras Mail* office; other eccentrics, wiser in their way, have built nests of wire, and in one case even of gold and silver spectacle frames. I have seen one bird which was vainly trying with its mate to construct a nest in one of the little round windows of the Economic and Art section of the Museum, soaking twigs in water, for what reason I cannot divine, unless he thought they would thereby become softer and stay in position, which he was not at all successful in getting them to do. The Crow evidently knows that water has a softening effect, for I have seen a bird come down to a tank with a piece of bread in his bill, put it into the water to soak, while he had a drink and then fly off with it. I have seen jackdaws also in the London Zoo do a similar thing. It is indeed curious to speculate on the extent of the Crow's intelligence. Sometimes, when flying, you will see him transfer something from his bill to his feet, and carry it thus a little way, as if he were trying to learn the kite's trick of using his feet for transport. Yet he never seems to learn to pick things off water with his feet, though picking objects up from that element at all is evidently an acquired trick with him. I noticed our Crows about the Museum are very poor hands at picking things off the tank, while the Hooghly Crows were quite handy at water work. Similarly, the Grand Hotel Crows are very good at catching flying, no doubt owing to constant feeding by residents there. The Crow's intelligence is of course kept up to a high level by the constant elimination of the young fools by death or capture; the *old* bird knows well the difference between a stick or umbrella and a gun. I have almost touched one with an umbrella and seen another suddenly recollect an appointment to a distant part of Calcutta on catching sight of a gun in my verandah. That a Crow should know a gun when he sees it, or that many birds should have a working acquaintance with the range of that weapon, is not so surprising a fact as might seem at first sight, for we must remember that birds have to learn by experience the appearance of their different natural enemies and the distance at which the proximity of each one becomes dangerous. Our Crow will pull at a kite's tail, or swoop on its back, out of pure light-heartedness and mischief; but he will not play tricks of that kind with a falcon, though he makes no secret of his hatred of the nobler bird. Similarly, I have seen Crows mobbing a tree-civet or toddy-cat, but although they made a great deal of noise, they took care to keep well out of reach; while with a dog they will go so far, I am told, as to tell off one of the fraternity to pull his tail when he is engaged with a bone, so that when the aggrieved canine turns round to snap, those in front can make off with his dinner. And this I can readily believe, as I have seen exactly the same trick played or attempted on a kite more than once; the Crows in the last cases I have observed seemed undoubtedly to be pairs, which accounts for their working together so well. No doubt the female does the tail-pulling, while the male takes the post of danger in front; in one instance I made sure of this from the forbearing behaviour of the Crow which had snatched the bone of contention, which he was able to do before any tail-pulling had taken place. I have alluded to the Crows annoying kites by way of recreation, and there is no doubt whatever that this is the object, just as they seem to take pleasure in letting a man come as near them as is consistent with safety. But they seem also to have regular games; at any rate I cannot otherwise account for the habit they have of assembling in the evening and playing what looks very like "I'm the king of the castle" on the Museum lightning-conductors, for the spiky top of these rods is not a pleasant seat for a Crow; and yet they are constantly trying to sit on them at this time.

The Crow on the whole must have a very happy life. He cannot want for food, for in addition to his natural prey of carrion and insects, he can pick up or steal all sorts of remnants of man's food; which makes it the more remarkable that his feeding habits are at times so unspeakably nasty. His enemies, outside man, who does not often get a chance at him, are few; and that the struggle for existence does not press him very hard seems obvious from the fact that he always has plenty of time to spare in annoying other creatures, from men to lizards. I have heard of a Crow watching one of those reptiles laying and eating up the eggs one by one! He is indeed a terrible pest to anything that is weak and helpless, though he often meets his match in a most unexpected way. I have seen him soundly beaten by the little spotted dove—about the last adversary one would expect him to fear—but a bad conscience no doubt makes him a coward.

What are his relations to the Jungle-crow (*Corvus macrorhynchus*) I do not know. Every now and then one hears, even in Calcutta, the provincial accents of this Mofussilite, and catches sight of him, easily distinguishable from the urban bird by his greater size and entirely black plumage. Is the smaller bird the master—not an unknown case among allied species—or is the size of the Jungle-crow a disadvantage to him when flying amongst buildings? At any rate, one has to get some distance away from Calcutta before one finds the big black Crow at all common. Yet he has a very wide range, from Gilgit where he meets the true raven with which he is sometimes confounded, to Siam and Singapore; and he is also the Crow of the Andamans, so that he must possess considerable powers of adapting himself to circumstances. But, from the fact that the Himalayan birds are the smallest and those from the Andamans and Burma the largest, we may infer that he likes a hot stuffy climate better than a cool bracing one. It is the other way with the true raven (*Corvus corax*), which is easily distinguished by his greater size and the beard of pointed hackles on his throat, for this bird is largest and finest in the hills and dwindles into a puny race when he lives in the plains; but he is always considerably bigger than the Jungle-crow.

Our familiar Calcutta friend is mostly confined to India, and to low elevations there, and does not seem to vary much in size, though in the drier parts his neck gets nearly white, and in Ceylon so much darker that it attracts the attention of any one who observes him; on the Burmese frontier he has a near relative in the Burmese House-crow (*Corvus insolens*) which is of the same size, but dark-necked and with a different note, but similar in habits. Outside India he has of late years been introduced as a scavenger into Zanzibar, where I first made his acquaintance in the wild state; but as a sanitary bird he is, in my opinion, much inferior to his hated rival, the kite. Moreover, there are, of course, Crows of other kinds in Africa, as there are in all the large divisions of the world except in South America, where the place of these birds is taken by the carrion hawks, which exhibit in their habits the combined rascality of Crow and kite. One of this group can often be seen at Zoological Gardens in the person of the Caracara hawk, a very handsome but cowardly and mischievous bird. It will be interesting to see what will happen when Crows at length gain a footing in South America, for some one is sure to introduce them sooner or later, just as our own rook (*Corvus frugilegus*) at home was lately his trial in South Africa. Of course indiscriminate introduction like this is much to be condemned from the point of view of the practical man, though from that of the naturalist it is of great interest, for future generations of observers will find in it an experiment in evolution.

Crows are certain to have an important influence on the fauna of a country, if only from their cunning and their long life. Whether Hesiod, when he said "Nine generations lives the croaking Crow" was strictly accurate is open to considerable doubt; the oldest Indian Crow I ever knew was at least fifteen and looked as young as ever he could have done. He was in the London Zoo, and I remember particularly that one very hard winter, although in an out-of-door aviary, he looked about the most cheerful bird in the gardens; so that if he haunts a warm climate here it is not because he cannot stand a cold one. There is no doubt that he feels the *heat* very badly, but he probably finds that an easy livelihood has compensating advantages.

I fear, indeed, that things are made too easy for him, for he is no doubt a deadly enemy to many smaller and more attractive birds, besides being a great nuisance to ourselves by his noise and pilfering, in which latter pursuit he will become appallingly impudent. When I used to encourage Crows, I remember one coming into my room after *chota-hazri*, taking a couple of mouthfuls out of the butter on my plate, and staying to wipe his beak on a pamphlet that lay handy before he sought the top of the *jillmill!* When you give him an inch he will take an ell, and my policy towards the Crows was one of war to the knife, for I think one pair to a compound is a fair working average. The Crows knew it, too, I think, for I was not popular with them; but for all that I would be the last to advocate the entire extermination of such a polished scoundrel as *Corvus splendens*.

Indian Magpie.
Dendrocitta rufa.

II.—THE MAGPIE.

"*Proud and pert as is a Pie.*"—*Chaucer.*

THE common Indian Magpie (*Dendrocitta rufa*) is certainly not the equal in pride and pertness of the European bird which Chaucer knew. For one thing it has less to be proud of, being soberly costumed in cinnamon and silver-grey instead of snow-white and glossy black like *Pica rustica* at home. Nor does it come down on the ground and swagger about there; its legs are very short, and restrict its movements to hopping on the very rare occasions when it does descend from the trees. Usually it keeps aloft, searching among the foliage for any small game that may present itself in the way of insects or young birds; and though conspicuous in its slow dipping flight from tree to tree, it is perhaps more often heard than seen. Its ordinary notes are certainly not more melodious than those of the home Magpie, one native name, "Handi-chancha" well expressing one of them; but it can produce some very pretty metallic sounds if it likes. Whether it can learn to talk I do not know; the natives, at all events, do not seem to make a pet of it, although one may now and then see the young birds on sale in the Bazaars. They may be known at once by their resemblance to their parents, though they are much lighter in colour, being buff instead of cinnamon. Of the old birds both sexes are alike, as is the rule among the crow tribe. At first sight the long-tailed, short-winged, and short-legged Indian Pie looks very different from the well-proportioned crow, none of whose members are unduly developed; but she has much the same character of cautious audacity, and, although not a "galley-ranger" like her black kindred, is very accommodating in appetite. Jerdon relates a case in which one used to daily visit a cage of small birds in a verandah, at first in order to eat the seed supplied to them; soon, however, he passed from petty larceny to murder, and was ultimately executed.

No doubt Pies, even more than crows, act as a healthy check on the exuberant domesticity of Philip Sparrow, which would otherwise overflow in those arboreal colonies in which his soul delights in safer localities than Calcutta. But Mag cannot be a very dangerous neighbour to most small birds, seeing that they flourish so well in our midst in spite of her presence and presumably not altogether disinterested enquiries into the progress of their home and family arrangements. She has no particular ill-wishers herself, for birds of the crow kind are seldom attacked by others, unless it be by the larger owls who steal upon them under cover of darkness; but the king-crow, in exercise of his office of supervisor of all doubtful characters in the feathered world, has been seen to harry her, clinging to her tail and being thus towed along for some distance. Whatever be the cause, although our Indian Magpie favours thorny twigs for building with, she does not, like the European bird, construct a dome with them over her nest, but sticks to the usual corvine pattern of an open cup. In the matter of eggs, however, she boldly defies convention, for she will have them with the pale ground colour tinted either pink or green, and enriched with spots varying in hue from bright red to dull brown. In respect to refreshments, on the other hand, besides exhibiting the family readiness to take whatever comes to hand, she is a true crow in having as frugal a mind as John Gilpin's wife, and in time of plenty will lay up stores for a rainy day. This I found out from the only specimen of the bird I ever kept, discovering that it had laid up bits of meat in various parts of its large cage soon ofter receiving the ration.

To whatever cause we may ascribe the result, the common Indian Pie is a very successful bird, and extends its range nearly all over the Empire from Cashmere to Tenasserim; and, although quite at home in the sweltering atmosphere of the plains, ascends the Himalayas up to 7,000 feet, and thrives particularly well there, hill specimens being of larger growth than those bred lower down. This is curious, for our cinnamon friend has a relative which is a thorough mountaineer, never living in the plains, though I have seen it as low down as Rajpore in the Doon. And this bird is smaller than the common one, although living under the same conditions in which its rival so adds to its stature. This hill Tree-pie (*Dendrocitta himalayensis*) is not so handsome a bird as its more widely distributed relative, its prevailing hue being a dark iron-grey.

Wherever our "wandering Pie"—as it is called in some books—goes in India, it will find poor relatives, much resembling itself in all but colour, which, for some reason or other, have failed to spread as *Dendrocitta rufa* has done. At present the problem defies solution ; but as the distribution of birds generally has been pretty well mapped out by this time, I hope the day is not far distant when ornithologists will begin to try and find out the reasons for it—why, for instance, one species of a genus should be able to live almost anywhere, as in the present case, while the others have bounds set to their wanderings.

The European Magpie, sometimes seen as a pet in Calcutta, where it has been imported from China, is another good case of a successful bird, for it is found all round the Northern Hemisphere, and is still extending its range, having invaded Ireland and become very common there even in human knowledge, though not by any means recently. Even in our Indian Empire it appears in Cashmere and Upper Burma, and the clan of Tree-pies may yet find in it a dangerous competitor, for a bird that is active both below and aloft has advantages which few possess.

A word seems needed for other exotic Magpies often seen in Calcutta as pets. These are the white-backed and black-backed Australian Magpies, better known in books as Piping Crows (*Gymnorhina leuconota* and *G. tibicen*). These are short-tailed pied birds, about the size of the common house-crow, and are quite as much allied to the shrikes as to the true crows, though they more closely resemble the latter in form and habits. They have and deserve a high reputation, for they are good and very free talkers, and their own natural note is a beautiful whistle, very different from the varied cacophony of the genuine Magpie and crow. It is not surprising, therefore, that they readily learn to whistle tunes, though in their case, as in our own, "a little knowledge" is objectionable. The London Zoo had one once which persistently whistled a line and a half of a song. With this, as the late Mr. A. Bartlett told me, he habitually saluted the morn, and got so annoying that he had to be banished from the precincts of the Superintendent's dwelling to the Western Aviary. For, as the narrator of the episode said, he "used to lie in bed and *sweat*, waiting for him to begin!"

Babbler.
Crateropus canorus.

III.—THE SEVEN SISTERS.

"*We are seven.*"—*Wordsworth.*

SOME years back, a new Viceroy was being shown the wonders of his temporary kingdom, and among these the Taj at Agra held, of course, an important place. Arrived before the glorious monument of Eastern love and pride, "the artless Aide-de-Camp was mute; the gilded staff were still" as Kipling says, in anxious expectation of the comment of His Excellency. But this, alas! when it came was merely the remark: "What are those funny little birds?" The shock must have been the greater for the fact that the mean fowls thus honoured were it seems, of that singularly disreputable species which is commonly known in India as the "Seven Sisters" or "Seven Brothers," or by the Hindustani equivalent of *sat-bhai*. In books it gets called the Jungle Babbler, the first part of the name being inappropriate, for it is found everywhere, and the last singularly happy, for it does babble with a vengeance. As may be inferred from their popular names, these birds go about in small packs of about half-a-dozen —there are not invariably seven, nor can these be a family party, since only three or four eggs are laid. They hop about searching for food on the ground or branches, murmuring squeakily to themselves meanwhile, and ever and anon burst out into a startling volley of wheezy hysterical chatter, which gets terribly upon one's nerves in time in a place where they are common. Linnæus, when he called the bird *Turdus canorus*, the tuneful thrush, must have been wildly ignorant of it, or have hopelessly mixed it up with an ally and a real songster, the huamei of China (*Trochalopterum canorum*), which he included under the same name. Modern ornithologists call our babbling brotherhood *Crateropus canorus*, placing them in a different family from the true thrushes, to which they nevertheless bear a strong general resemblance in form and size. But the differences are very soon perceptible if one studies the living birds. Your thrush is sleek, stiff, and starch; he is a musical artist, but allows himself no artistic license in his dress, which is neat to primness. The Babblers, on the contrary, have a fluffy, frowsy appearance; their tails hang loosely, and their wings, which are short, are not neatly tucked up as they should be, but lie anyhow. Nor have they the excuse of pleasing colour, such as many clumsy birds can boast of; a brownish grey, of "unparalleled dignitude" as Baboo Jabberjee would say, is almost the only hue visible in their attire, and is not particularly well set off by a white eye like a jackdaw's and whitish legs and bill of an unpleasantly anæmic appearance. There is, however, a real interest attaching to these disreputable-looking birds. We are all familiar with Lamb's appallingly ugly lady whose facial turpitude was supposed to be atoned for by the possession of superlative moral excellence; and unquestionably fraternal affection is the strong point of the babbling brotherhood. In the grave pages of the Asiatic Society's Journal a friend of mine has recorded his frequent experience of the devoted courage with which these feeble-winged creatures will rush to the defence of a comrade held in the grip of a trained hawk; on one occasion the victim was actually rescued by its comrades before the hawk could receive its master's assistance, and on another, one of the Babblers was caught by hand as it clung to the back of its relative's murderer. No one, so far as I am aware, has recorded behaviour anything like this on the part of our song-thrush (*Turdus musicus*), who appears to be rather a coward, although his near relative the missel-thrush (*Turdus viscivorus*) will show fight boldly in defence of his home and mate. And with regard to these Babblers courage appears to be a variable quality even in this particular species; for Dr. Jerdon expressly states that the Jungle Babbler will *not* attack a trained hawk flown at the flock as the bolder Mahratta Babbler (*Argya malcolmi*) will. Dehra Dun, therefore, where the above incident occurred, must be inhabited by a peculiarly warlike clan of *Crateropus canorus*, and certainly they are very numerous there and obtrusively noisy. That sociability is a passion with the species no one who has studied it can doubt; I have kept several, and have found that they almost invariably exhibited the spirit of the poet's goldfinch, who

> "*A prison with a friend preferred*
> *To liberty without.*"

If one found himself outside the cage which contained the happy family, he "did his possible" to get in again without any thought of escape. It may be ungenerously suggested that such birds are afraid to go about alone, lest their ribald remarks, made in the security of numbers, meet with a just retaliation at the beaks and claws of outraged bird society; and so it may be, but nevertheless there is a well-spring of sincere sociability under the Babbler's frowsy feathering. On the comparatively rare occasions when my captives were still, they employed themselves in affectionately tickling each other's heads as they cuddled together, and I have even seen one diligently employed in endeavouring to clean the wing of a friend, soiled by the bird lime with which its capture had been effected. At the same time it must be admitted that the addition to their ordinary diet of table scraps of such a delicacy as a cock-roach was apt to produce a sad disruption of fraternal harmony. On such occasions one might see one brother prone in the sand, while another, holding his head "in chancery" with one foot, was punching the same with his beak in a manner calculated to awake grave fears for the integrity of the sufferer's skull when the punishment should be over; and once I saw two birds adherent with bill and claw to one and the same cockroach, which a third was devouring, as neither of the joint owners dared to let go his hold! These traits of character would seem to show that *Crateropus canorus* is in about the same stage of moral evolution as that represented by the public school boy, a gallant defender of his kind against the assaults of "cads," "nippers," and "vulgar plebs" generally, but inclined also to be severe on them in individual disputes.

The reason for the development of such clannishness is obvious when the very weak flight of this bird is noticed; the short wings are beaten quickly for a short distance, and the labour is economised by a gliding skim till a fresh effort is required; and with such a method of flight escape by aërial evolutions is very much at a discount. On his feet the Babbler is much more at home, and hops along with considerable speed, never running smoothly as the true thrushes often do. He differs from these birds also in another noticeable point in the use of the feet, having the crow-like habit of using them to hold anything large he is eating—a thing no thrush would stoop to do—or think of doing, more likely. Babblers also resemble crows and differ from most thrushes in the young birds being like their parents; young thrushes being, as everyone knows, much more spotted than old ones. Whether the Babblers go through any elaborate courtship ceremony I cannot say; male and female are equally ugly, but this does not prevent some birds from making themselves ridiculous before the object of their affections, and possibly these are among the number—a Babbler could not be dignified if he tried. Their nest is just about the sort of abode one would expect them to build, a simple cup, more or less loose and untidy, placed almost anywhere in shrubs or trees. But the eggs are the one beautiful thing about the bird, being of that lovely blue so noticeable in the hedge-sparrow's at home, and very glossy in addition. As above implied the young ones fledge off very like the old, but they have dark brown instead of white eyes. A very plump one I experimentally ate tasted much like a quail, and herein perhaps lies an economic possibility for the "Seven Sisters;" the clan would just about fill a pie. The French in Algeria regard the local babbler there (*Argya fulva*) as *gibier*, but their notions in that matter are known to be liberal; witness the colonists in New Caledonia who used to eat the local crow, until one day a native asked one of these sportsmen why the white men ate what *they* religiously avoided, giving as a reason, when questioned, that the said crows *ate them* when exposed dead on platforms in the forest according to custom. After this crow ceased to figure in the Colonial *menu*.

The said Algerian Babbler is the nearest of the family to Europe, and generally speaking, babblers inhabit Africa and the Oriental region only. Our familiar suburban friend, which is found all over India, is the only one about here in a wild state, though several of his more or less close relatives may be met with at bird-dealer's places, including the abovementioned huamei of China, recognizable by its russet plumage and white eyebrows, and another species common to that country and Further India, the slate-coloured, white-cheeked Chinese mocking-bird or peko (*Dryonastes chinensis*), which, though obviously of the vulgar babbler family, is a finer songster than almost any bird I have heard, and a mocker to boot. Some day, possibly, when people begin to realize that desirable birds can be cultivated in gardens as well as desirable plants (the efforts of humanity in the former direction hitherto having been largely expended in the acclimatization of nuisances) we may have the peko making our gardens melodious and supplanting the "shrieking sisterhood" altogether—a consummation devoutly to be wished, although, till some such better bird takes their place, their industriously insectivorous habits may give them a *raison d'être.*

Common Bengal Bulbul.
Molpastes bengalensis.

IV.—THE BULBUL.

"*The Bulbul, which did chase the jewelled butterflies.*"—*Arnold.*

CONSIDERING what a charming and characteristic feature butterflies form in the tropical landscape, it would not be much to the Bulbul's credit if chasing them were his most noteworthy occupation. Undoubtedly he does catch butterflies sometimes, for I once saw a wild Bulbul with one in his bill—not "jewelled," but plain white—and he will eat them readily enough in confinement. But on the other hand, fruit is undoubtedly his more ordinary food; a certain *Lantana* bush I wot of is much resorted to by both Bulbuls and butterflies, and the berries seem to be the birds' only object in visiting it. And captive Bulbuls display an indiscriminateness in taste as regards the species of butterflies they devour, that would shock many of the exponents of "warning colouration in insects;" eating, without the stimulus of hunger, species which other birds will avoid unless they have no choice allowed. This may be interpreted in two ways. Either the Bulbul is such a common bird because he doesn't care what he eats; or he is a mere amateur in butterfly-eating, and doesn't know what's good, like a young bird who has his experience to gain. Certainly his insect-catching when at liberty is mostly concerned with smaller game, for it is not always easy to see what he takes when he rises in the air a short distance and then drops back to his perch. For he is a bird of varied abilities; he can skip about gracefully among the branches of a shrub, though he is more given to sitting on the top; and on the wing his movements, though not particularly powerful or swift, are easy and graceful to a degree. Only on the ground is he awkward, for his legs are too short for him to hop with much agility or keep his tail clear; but he does not often descend to earth, and wisely. No small bird looks well on the ground unless he can run, like the wagtail, and even then he is rather insignificant. But place the Bulbul as one generally sees him, on a lofty spray, his jetty crest erect, and his tail drooping in a *négligé* manner all his own, and it is difficult to find a small bird so picturesque. True, his black fore-quarters fade off to dusty brown on the wings and iron-grey on the breast, and the only bright colour he boasts is the silky crimson patch modestly concealed under the root of his tail; but even so he is more strikingly attired than most

European birds. Both cock and hen are also equally well dressed; but the young are duller and look rather shabby, especially as they have to wear a rusty-buff escutcheon instead of a blood-red one. This curiously-placed bit of colour seems a family feature with Bulbuls; it is always either red or yellow, however, when it occurs at all, other tints being strictly barred. The only Bulbul which occurs in Europe—in the Cyclades—bears a yellow patch, being otherwise of a snuffy brown; and this is possibly the bird which has got mixed up with the Nightingale in Eastern poetry, as it occurs in Palestine, and is there called Bulbul by the Arabs. Bulbul in Persian is always supposed to mean the true Nightingale, the lover of the rose, and there seems to be no reason to doubt the correctness of the identification—though it may be mentioned that the Persian nightingale (*Daulias golzii*) is not absolutely identical with the European bird. More to the point are the facts that the Yarkandis call the Barred Warbler (*Sylvia nisoria*) the Bulbul, and that the Palestine Bulbul (*Pycnonotus xanthopygus*) above alluded to is a really fine singer. So that whatever bird was called by the name to start with, it seems to be about as indefinite among Orientals as "Mocking-bird" and "Sparrow" are in our own language. However, in India "Bulbul" is taken by both natives and Europeans in a very definite signification for a large group of pretty birds, of which our dark Bengal species (*Molpastes bengalensis*) may very fairly claim to be the type. He certainly is not much of a songster, but his notes are never harsh and always singularly cheerful and liquid, conveying an unequivocal sense of happiness and well-being; and he is a thoroughly *nice* bird. He is not obtrusively sociable nor peevishly solitary and quarrelsome; when the natives make him fight, it is by showing two hungry birds a morsel of food, over which of course there is a conflict. It is for this purpose that he is so often kept tame, tied to a cloth-padded, T-shaped iron perch by a long string connected with a soft thread round his body. Fortunately, he does not seem to get much damaged in these fights, and at the end of the winter, the bulbul-fighting season, he is released, unless he has proved himself an exceptional champion and worth reserving for future triumphs. It is a shame to make use of his courage in this way, for he is really a plucky bird, and will even beat off a crow from his nest, although not more than half as large again as a sparrow himself. The said nest is an open one placed in a bush, and has nothing particularly remarkable about it. The eggs, however, are very pretty, being pinky-white with red spots, a common colour in the family. Young Bulbuls taken just as their tails begin to grow are easily reared and become very tame, making most charming pets; I had one which was allowed full liberty, and was at times quite a nuisance by its determination to follow me about. The Bulbul, indeed, seems to have a warm heart, although as above noted not fussily affectionate with its kind; a well known English authority on cage birds has recorded that a male Bulbul in his possession had his paternal instincts so quickened by witnessing the rearing of a brood of American Blue Robins (*Sialia sialis*) in the same aviary that he insisted on taking a helping hand, and even murderously attacked the real father for not altogether resigning in his favour. This, indeed, might be considered as carrying matters rather too far, but after all the poor bird was no worse than any other "well meaning person."

Red-whiskered Bulbul.
Otocompsa emeria.

I have never noticed what are the exact relations, friendly or otherwise, between the black Bulbul and his smaller relative the Red-whiskered (*Otocompsa emeria*) which is also not uncommon here. The Red-whiskered Bulbul is not nearly so numerous, and is easily distinguished by his white breast and throat, and by having his red under-tail-patch reproduced on his cheeks in two small scarlet tufts. Besides he is considerably smaller, and has a much longer crest, elegantly tapered to a point. Altogether he is a very pretty little bird, and one which would attract attention anywhere. He has a much wider range than the larger Bulbul, extending from India to Siam and China, while the other species is not found outside this country, and is confined here to the north-east, being replaced elsewhere by other species very much resembling it, but not so big or so black. In Western and Southern India the Red-whiskered Bulbul also gives place to another species, which is however, very like it, chiefly differing in having no white tip to the tail. Both of our Bulbuls must be fairly hardy birds, for they range up the Himalayas to quite a temperate climate; however, they no doubt come down in the winter just like human visitants to the hills—which is where a hill-bird has such an advantage over one that has to make a long migration on the level.

I have seen variations of both our species of Bulbuls; in the case of the larger one the "freak" was ash-grey and in the smaller, white, the red markings persisting in each case, as indeed red colour usually does in albino varieties. Both "sports" were very pretty, and as Bulbuls will breed in confinement, they would be well worth taking some trouble to perpetuate. But no one is likely to take that trouble in India, and Bulbuls are not very commonly kept at home, although both of our species can be obtained there at more or less moderate prices. The Bulbul, unfortunately for its reputation for a cage-bird, has only beauty of form to recommend it, and the home fancier demands a song or gaudy colour if he is to honour a non-seed-eating bird with a place in his aviaries, with the occasional variation of "starring it" on the show bench.

V.—THE KING-CROW

"I am monarch of all I survey."—*Cowper.*

THE King-Crow, or Drongo as he is called in books, has a wide enough kingdom to rule over, extending from West Africa to China, and here in India he may claim to be one of our most characteristic birds, for it would hardly be an exaggeration to say that there is one of these jet-black fork-tailed birds between every two telegraph posts for many miles of country. Where there are no telegraph-wires the king-crow will put up with a dead branch or a cow's back; he wants some perch that will afford a clear outlook and plenty of room for evolutions around it, and though sometimes, as on the *maidan,* he will sit about on the ground, he is grievously falling from the traditions of his family in so doing, for the Drongos generally are as much given to pride of place as the green pigeon, concerning which native traditions avers that when it comes down to drink it carries a twig in its feet, lest its enemies should say that it had ever deigned to leave a perch. Perhaps our common Drongo (*Dicrurus ater*) owes his prosperity to waiving his family pride, since even settling to catch prey is contrary to strict Drongo etiquette, and he is constantly doing this, though he is active enough at taking insects on the wing. But he is by way of being a very versatile bird, and though he appears never to touch vegetable food, he has been known to take small birds as well as insects, and even to capture small fish ; a feat of which no one will deem him incapable who has seen him taking his bath by plunges like a swallow, a method of performing ablutions much favoured by birds which are ready of wing. And the King-Crow is remarkably good at aërial evolutions, whence he is enabled to maintain that authority over birds great and small which the Deccanis have neatly expressed by calling him *kotwal*, superintendent of police. Armed with very punishing beak and claws, he is a terror to evil-doers like the kite and crow, who cannot catch him, much as they would like to—I have seen a *sickly* King-Crow fall a prey to a kite—but also, it is to be regretted, at times a nuisance to the more peaceful portion of the bird community, robbing them when he can of their insect prey ; although perhaps he feels that this is merely an exaction of a tribute due to his energetic exertions against the criminal classes, which the public would churlishly withhold.

It must be admitted that he is sometimes very unscrupulous; a King-Crow has been known to give the alarm of a hawk in order to frighten off a bird which was capturing an insect which he wanted himself, though such an action shows intelligence of no mean order ; and also exemplifies the vocal powers of the King-Crow, which, like many other birds possessed of a powerful and flexible voice, has considerable aptitude for variations. His notes are very pleasant, and he is almost the earliest bird to tune up in the morning. The male and female King-Crows are quite alike, and even the young are fledged black at first, though afterwards they become mottled with white below, and it is years before this marking disappears altogether. The eggs that give them birth are very pretty, being salmon-coloured spotted with red, though pure white ones are not uncommon. They are deposited in an open nest in a tree, which the parents vigorously defend; but these, with all their care, are liable to be imposed upon by a remarkable cuckoo (*Surniculus lugubris*), which is one of the very best instances of mimicry in nature, since it resembles the Drongo, not only in size, but in colour and form, having a forked tail, an altogether exceptional feature in the cuckoo family. No doubt the impostor benefits in a general way by resembling a bird which is given to making itself respected by others, but the special advantage secured is probably greater security in foisting its unwelcome offspring on the Drongos; this, however, it does not always accomplish successfully, for an instance has been recorded in which the unfortunate cuckoo was actually seen to be pecked to death by them.

I am not aware that this Drongo-cuckoo is found about Calcutta, but this may possibly be the case, as it is no doubt often passed over as a King-Crow; but anyone who notices one of these which looks a little different from the rest, and on watching it finds that it has the toes in pairs after cuckoo fashion, will know that he has seen a specimen of the mimic.

There is one thing about the King-Crow that puzzles me considerably. Very often I have noticed that one of the forks of the tail is much worn away; whether the right or the left I have not observed, nor can I suggest an explanation—unless it is that the bird when sitting on a bough or wire and turning round always does so on the same side, so as to bring all the consequent friction on one-half of the tail. The King-Crow's tail, indeed, seems rather an unwieldy member, for he does not lift it up in the air when on the ground, where it must be rather in his way, and although a forked tail is undoubtedly meant as an aid to evolution in flight, in our present subject it seems unnecessarily long, and from its turned-up edges looks as if it were quite as much for ornament as for use.

The whole family of Drongos have more or less forked tails; this and their almost invariably black plumage easily distinguishing them from their near relatives, the shrikes, of which a typical representative may be seen in Calcutta gardens in the person of the Brown Shrike (*Lanius cristatus*) a bull-headed, black-eyebrowed bird rather larger than a sparrow, given to making highly unpleasant noises and very appreciative of cockroaches thrown out for him. Both shrikes and Drongos have the habit of holding their food in one foot like a parrot, but the latter are not known to impale their prey like the former. No Drongos are found outside the old world, but in general domineering their place is ably filled in America by the king-bird and other members of the American family of tyrant-flycatchers. In Europe no bird seems to have taken up this position, though the missel-thrush attempts it a little. Perhaps the European birds are too free and independent to be thus lorded over, or possibly the supply of insects is not suitable for the support of birds which, although as big as thrushes, do not hunt for their prey, but like Mr. Micawber, wait for something to turn up and then come down on it, as is the custom of these Oriental and American oligarchs in feathers. The true shrikes, one would think, might fill such a place, but they prefer devouring their smaller relatives to waging war on birds of prey, though they hate them well enough. I have only noticed one near relative of the King-Crow about Calcutta, and that in the Botanical Gardens, in the person of the Kesraj or Hair-crested Drongo (*Chibia hottentotta*), a larger species than the King-Crow, with a shorter tail and longer bill, and exquisitely glossy plumage, deriving its English name from the curious ornament of a few long hairs springing from the forehead. This bird is sociable, unlike the common Drongo, and does not go in much for fly-catching, preferring to rummage in flowers for honey and insects, for which purpose its long, curved, fine-pointed bill is well adapted—it is. in fact, a drongo trying to turn honeysucker. Another cousin of the King-Crow's, however, although only known here as a captive, cannot be passed over. This is the Bhimraj, or Racket-tailed Drongo (*Dissemurus paradiseus*), a bird nearly as big as a magpie, with the outer tail-feathers prolonged for about a foot into long bare shafts, with a bit of feathering at the tip—an ornament which does not usually stand much chance of maintaining its perfection in the miserably small cages in which the poor birds are usually confined. No wonder they do not live long; very few, I am told, survive a year. But given a big cage, say three or four feet square, the bhimraj is not difficult to keep; he will eat almost anything, like one of the crow tribe, though the more live insects he gets the better; and a lizard he will tear to pieces with a positively fiendish joy. He is, however, a very sociable bird, extremely fond of being noticed and petted, and is the most accomplished mimic in existence. The neigh of a horse, the mew of a cat, and the song of a canary, he will render in perfection, and has even been known to talk—an accomplishment not recorded, so far as I am aware, of the famous American Mocking-bird. To any one who wants a really good pet bird, I can cordially recommend the bhimraj.

VI.—THE TAILOR-BIRD.

"*Singer and Tailor am I.*"—*Kipling.*

HEREIN, and in the pretty stanza that follows, our poet sadly flatters the Tailor-bird, for any one who waits to hear "durzee" sing will have much the same experience as Mark Twain's young pilgrim in Palestine, who was discovered waiting patiently for a vocal effort on the part of a mud-turtle, on the strength of the text "the voice of the turtle is heard in the land." Singer our small cock-tailed friend is not, though his note is something astonishing for loudness, and gives reason, as has been justly remarked, for thankfulness that the elephant does not possess a voice in like proportion. *Orthotomus sutorius*, however, doubtless feels that as the only member of the melodious family of warblers commonly seen about here, it is due to his position to make his presence felt. So, when the spirit moves him, he shouts "to-whee, to-whee, to-whee," with such vigour that he gets black on the side of the neck, having a cunningly concealed patch of that colour there which only shows when he is calling. Mrs. Durzee, no doubt, admires both hue and cry, for, unlike most of our warblers at home, Durzee goes in for conspicuous superiority to his mate, at any rate in the breeding season, for then he alone sports a tail about twice the usual length, and elegantly tapered off. Except for this, the

Tailor-bird is in build very like our English wren, and were it brown, instead of green above and white below, might pass for one with a hasty observer, especially as its habits are very similar; it is generally solitary, and equally lively on its legs when hopping on bush or lawn, and weak on the wing when it trusts itself to flight. Like "Jenny," too, our sartorial artist is insectivorous, and will tackle insects of good size, though he relies on his bill alone to manipulate them. This makes it the more remarkable that he is able to build the wonderful nest which gives him his name and his reputation. A bird which puts its foot to a thing, as the even more clever weaver-bird does, has a great advantage over one which has but one instrument to work with. But probably both of the tailors work at their wonderful structure, which is simply a big living leaf, or several, actually *sewn* into a rough bag for the reception of the inner nest, with silk or fibre somehow procured by the bird, passed through holes bored in the leaves by its slender bill, and finished off at the end with what is said to be a knot. The nests vary very much in construction as far as the details of tailoring are concerned; there may be, as above implied, one leaf or many pressed into the service, and the thread may be of cobweb, cocoon-silk, vegetable fibre, or real sewing-thread pilfered from a verandah; for the Tailor-bird is one of the most familiar of our birds, and is to be seen even in town, tamely hopping about pot-plants a few feet from a room.

Nevertheless, though broods have been often brought off in the Museum compound, I have never seen the nest *in situ*, and it is naturally not easy to find. There is a good specimen of a single-leaf nest in the Museum for any one to see who has not met with an actual specimen; but the Tailor-bird's reputation is a century old in Europe, and many people must have seen pictures giving more or less of an idea of it and its abode. The young birds are cradled for the most part in cotton-wool, of which the inner nest is composed, and when they come out in the world are charmingly tame little things, with a very strong likeness to their parents, except that the chestnut cap which marks the old birds is not so bright in the young; although in many warblers the young birds are actually brighter than their parents while keeping the same pattern.

The eggs are, according to Mr. Hume, from whom I take my details about the nests, most remarkably variable, for although always spotted with reddish brown, they may have either a white or a bluish-green ground colour. But as these two types do not occur in the same nest, it is very probable that the disposition to produce eggs of one or other colour "runs in the family" in certain strains of Tailor-birds, just as a common duck has been known to secure her destruction and that of her descendants (who took after her) by laying eggs which always had *yolks* of the very unappetising appearance of melted glue! There are only three or four in the clutch, so that Durzee has not to work so hard for the family as Jenny Wren, who is wont to resemble the traditional old lady who lived in a shoe in the exuberance of her family. Presumably the reason for the difference in two so similar birds is that the hanging cradle won't accommodate safely more than a very limited number of infants, while the wren's nest in a hedge can be packed with impunity. Besides, the bitter struggle for existence in a cold climate requires a considerable prolificacy to keep a small weak species going against many risks. Now, though Durzee has doubtless a great many ill-wishers, his food-supply is never likely to fail, nor is it ever cold enough in his home to nip the smallest bird, seeing that he only inhabits warm climates, not ascending our hills more than 4,000 feet, and only ranging, outside India, into Burma, Siam, and South China. Needless to say, he is not a migratory bird, and any day at all seasons his tiny form may be noticed in our gardens even in the middle of the town. Here, then, is an opportunity for any of our amateur naturalists. It is doubtful if every detail of the building of Durzee's nest has ever been watched, as it has in the case of our other wonderful architect, the weaver; and any one who can locate a pair of Tailor-birds in his or her compound, and, penetrating into their secrets, tell us exactly how the thing is done, they will be doing a service to ornithology; so much is there to study even in our commonest birds here, for India is the home of wonderful nest-builders There are other warblers in the tailoring trade besides *Orthotomus*, and curiously enough these also are non-migratory birds of insignificant vocal attainments; the migratory warblers, who do most of the warbling, like our blackcap (*Sylvia atricapilla*) at home, being nothing out of the way as architects. Darwin has observed that beauty and the power of song seem to a great extent to replace each other; the songlessness of beautiful birds is almost proverbial. And similarly songsters do not seem to run to architecture, and *vice versâ*; the tailor and weaver are more remarkable for noise than melody, and the nightingale, with twenty centuries of reputation for music, is but a poor nest-constructor compared with many humbler birds. Another curious fact is that clever birds of any sort display the infirmities of genius in a most marked way by having nasty tempers; song birds are generally solitary, and a weaver colony admirably exemplifies the definition of a sociable animal as one which always sits within quarrelling distance of another. I fear that Durzee, although belonging to a profession usually credited with peaceful proclivities, comes under this indictment. He is certainly only about the ninth part of a bird, but one never sees two Tailor-birds together, unless they are husband and wife or members of a family; and oftener the little artist is alone. Herein probably is the reason why with habits so well calculated to preserve his species, he is not more common; two of a trade never agree, and Durzee, like Cock Robin, has doubtless long ago learnt that a private pitch is the first necessity of life, and that after a time even the little apprentices must be compelled to move into the next street.

VII.—THE ORIOLE.

"*There's a golden bird.*"—*Hood.*

GOLDEN indeed is the rich plumage of our Black-headed Oriole (*Oriolus melanocephalus*), and the prevailing hue is admirably set off by the black hood, wings and tail; while the pink bill and grey feet add prettily contrasting details to the whole. This fulness of beauty is most characteristic of the old cock; for young birds at first have the yellow body much paler and streaked with black, and the black-head, to equalize matters, duller and streaked with yellow. The bill is also black, and altogether, although as birds go rather showy, they are not to be compared to their father. Their mother may be like them, if she is still a young thing, but only then. For among the happy birds good looks do not deteriorate with age, and in some cases the gentler sex become much more beautiful with advancing years. And this is one of them; for the hen Orioles become in course of time almost as brilliant as their mates, merely showing a tinge of green at times in the yellow—but the change in their case does not take place so early in life. It is curious to see how Nature is continually striving to bring the hen bird up to her mate's level of beauty; for the progressive increase of beauty in the hen occurs in several groups, notably in the hawks, This is quite a different thing from the assumption of male plumage by hen birds which by age or accident have become barren, such as often occurs among hen pheasants; and can only be ascribed to a natural tendency on the part of the species to progress in a given direction, the male leading the way.

This is well seen in our domestic birds. If we ornament an unoffending bird such as the Chinese goose or the pigeon with a knob on its nose, we find the male grows a bigger one. If, on the other hand, Nature has been beforehand with us in bestowing the decorations, such as the comb and wattles of the fowl and the bare red face of the Muscovy duck, and we take the birds into domestication, we find that the females, in which these decorations were rudimentary or absent, proceed to develop them in imitation of their lords, quite independently of our selection. And if we deliberately breed for big-combed fowls, the hens will run the cocks very close indeed in the matter of head-dress.

But to get back to our Orioles; their young are cradled in an excellent nest, cup-shaped and firmly laced into a fork high up in a tree, and they emerged from white eggs spotted with black, this type of egg being a family one with them. They feed on fruit and insects, and are thorough tree-birds, never seen on the ground, and not making themselves conspicuous when perched. The chief indication of the Oriole's presence among us is his beautiful liquid whistle, and the occasional appearance of the bird in his leisurely flight from one tree to another. Such are the habits of Orioles in general, and they seem a thriving race, for they spread from Australia to the British Isles, where one species, the Golden Oriole (*Oriolus galbula*), an even more beautiful bird than the subject of this article, has bred, but cannot establish itself on account of persecution. This Oriole is a rare winter-visitor to our North-West, but has a resident relative ranging all over India, which closely resembles it—the yellow-headed mango-bird (*Oriolus kundoo*). Both have yellow instead of black heads, and only differ in some slight details of marking, and in the fact that the migratory bird has, as one would expect, longer wings. I don't remember ever seeing this mango-bird in Calcutta, but it is very likely to occur here. The black-headed species has an even wider range than the Indian Golden Oriole, for it extends into Burma as far as Tenasserim. In Southern India and Ceylon it gets smaller and has the black wings less varied with yellow than is the case here; but Orioles do not give much scope for variation—they are just yellow and black birds as a rule, and there is an end of it. It is a curious fact that, although their food seems simple enough, Orioles don't bear confinement well, our black-headed one especially, and one seldom sees them caged. Our only species which is not black and yellow, the Maroon Oriole (*Oriolus traillii*) of the hills, is an exception and will thrive and keep in good condition where the golden birds would be miserable scare-crows. Although the Orioles have such a wide range in the Old World, they have never penetrated into the New, the American birds commonly so called really belonging to a very different family, the Troupials. They reproduce the real Oriole colours and patterns to a remarkable extent, but are different in form and habits, being in these respects somewhat intermediate between a starling and a weaver-bird, while the real Orioles have a form and style peculiarly their own. It must be confessed that the American birds are much more interesting; they also tend to range northwards more than do the Old World Orioles, and hence help to enliven the United States to a very great extent, some of most brilliant and common birds there belonging to this troupial family. We might have more brilliant birds in England if we could only let them alone; I have already alluded to the persecution of our one Oriole, and even the green woodpecker is oftener seen in a bird stuffer's shop window than on a tree in the open! As the Oriole is one of the brightest birds I am dealing with, I may perhaps be allowed to conclude with an earnest appeal to all Anglo-Indians to help in the preservation of beautiful birds, which exist in every country under difficulties, both from natural enemies and from man. The plain-coloured species can take care of themselves out here at any rate; but beauty is everywhere a fatal gift to the lower animals, and it is very much to be hoped that the recent enactment will preserve against the export of skins the more brilliant kinds whose danger is the greatest. Even about Calcutta we have in the larger kingfisher, the blue-jay, the golden-backed woodpecker, and the subject of the present chapter, a quartette of birds which would attract attention anywhere, and going further afield fresh showy species present themselves, too numerous to mention in few words. Posterity would not have thought much of us as a cultured nation if we had allowed such creatures to be hunted to extermination in countries under our rule, when so many centuries ago Alexander the Great—in India on a mere military expedition—gave orders that the peafowl should not be molested, through admiration of their beauty alone.

Common Mynah.
Acridotheres tristis.

VIII.—THE MYNAH.

"*I am not black in my heart, though yellow in my legs..*"
—*Shakespeare.*

THE Mynah needs perhaps to make some apology for his yellow stockings, since such mustard-coloured understandings are not usual among small birds, pertaining rather to the rapacious tribe, and being thus a badge of anything but respectability. But the Mynah atones for his yellow legs, feet, and face, by the exceedingly decorous plumage which covers the rest of him; no objection can be made to his black hood, or the sober chocolate of his body colour, or to the plain black, diversified with white, of his quills and tail. It is no wonder that Linnæus, probably having only seen a Mynah stuffed, and concluding from his general style that he was some poor relation of the Bird of Paradise, called him *Tristis*, the sad-coloured, for as a *Paradisea* he did not show up well. He has long, however, been degraded to his proper rank among the starlings, and named with a happiness somewhat rare amongor nithologists. *Acridotheres*—the grasshopper-catcher—and so he is likely to remain *Acridotheres tristis* till the end of the chapter (the general rule being that a bird always bears the first specific name bestowed on it). Nevertheless as a starling our present subject is a rather big and showy bird, being certainly equal in looks to any of his relatives in Calcutta, none of which bear the shot-silk sheen of green and purple which adorns the home starling, also a visitor to India. For the starlings or Mynahs are in great force in the East, which is their true home, and the common Mynah is a good type of the clan. Bold, vigorous, and pushing, he secures to himself a large share of all good things in the way of insects and fruit that may be going, and is a bird of remarkably all-round abilities, though not particularly graceful in his movements. On the ground he runs and walks well, hopping when he wants to put on an extra spurt, albeit there is a swing in his gait which is not particularly elegant. No doubt, however, he is proud of this, as it is a family character; geese, which do not suffer from excessive modesty, have a similar style of going, and are known to be redoubtable pedestrians in their quiet way. But the Mynah, unlike many ground-birds, is nimble and active in a tree as well; and his flight, though not remarkably fast, is tolerable enough for ease, and he feels sufficient confidence in it to occasionally attempt a little insect-catching on the wing, when his quarry has got away from him on foot. When he flies, he tucks up his long yellow shanks to his breast, showing conclusively that birds which stow their legs this way when on the wing do so by custom, not for convenience; for from their size one would think that he would do better to stow them astern like the paddy-bird and other waders. The Mynah, like most of the birds I have dealt with, goes in for equality between the sexes in the matter of dress. You can only tell a hen Mynah by her slightly smaller form, and by her exemption from the amorous fits which impel her spouse to now and then puff himself out and bow grotesquely for her edification, meanwhile emitting various gurglings, presumably meant to please her ear; the result being charmingly uncertain, for with Mynahs as with men apparently

A glance of despair is no guide,
It may have its ridiculous side,
It may draw you a tear,
Or a box on the ear,
You can never be sure till you've tried.

At least I judge this to be the case from having seen a Mynah pecked by his spouse for showing off, and also the lady become suddenly kind for the same reason apparently. The gentler sex in Mynahs have no particular reason to make themselves too cheap, for I have observed no less than three cocks bowing and scraping after one hen, and doubtless amatory rivalry will often account for the savage contests in which one sometimes sees Mynahs indulge. In other cases the possession of an eligible nesting site will furnish a reason, for, like other birds that nest in holes, the Mynah is sometimes hard put to it for house-room. I remember once seeing a mynah-fight in which two, no doubt the heads of families, lay clenched as to their feet upon the ground, while what were no doubt their wives looked on together with certain crows, who had evidently been attracted, like Mark Twain and his friends in Italy on a similar occasion, by a disinterested desire to be allowed "to help cord up the dead." The crows, however, were not officious beyond a nervous twitch at a combatant's tail, for the Mynah is a good bird of his hands, so to speak, and can make himself respected even by a crow; indeed, the Market Sergeant told me that he had once seen a crow nearly pecked to death by a pair of these birds. The Mynah is indeed a truly respectable character; while offering a creditable resistance to aggression, he does not seem, as a rule, to interfere with other birds, though I have seen him clinging to the entrance of a sparrow's nest in a manner that betokened designs either on the babies or the bedding; I fear possibly the former, since I have noticed a small house-lizard in a Mynah's bill, and from such a victim to a young bird is not a very long step. At the same time, a Mynah likes a warm nest, so perhaps a desire to borrow a little upholstery was the real motive. The Mynah's eggs are of a cheerful light blue, like those of most starlings, and his young, when fledged, are like himself, but less brightly and distinctly marked. I have seen young birds with *brown* heads, which may be either a "sport" or the result of the softer plumage of the young getting sooner rusty on that part. Mr. Aitken in Hume's "Nest and Eggs of Indian Birds," gives an interesting account of a pair of Mynahs which in every alternate brood produced a *white* young one. I have seen several white Mynahs myself; one in particular which Mr. Rutledge had was very interesting, having assumed its natural colour at the first moult—a contingency which is always possible with albinos unless they have pink eyes. On one occasion also I saw a bird in the Bazaar with pale cinnamon body-plumage, and once the skin of one such was submitted to me, which showed a change to the normal colour actually going on by moult. Abnormalities in Mynah complexion, therefore, may often be set down to individual weakness of constitution; but the Mynah is a vigorous bird as a rule, and given to enlarging his borders as a species. Most of the Indian Empire, from Kashmir to Mergui, is held by him, and he ascends the hills up to a very temperate climate, though I was assured on good authority that he had only penetrated to Darjeeling within the last twenty years. Outside India man has helped him to a settlement in the Andamans, Australia, New Zealand, and Honolulu, but he is a bird which should be introduced into a new country with caution, as he is too powerful and too free a breeder to be allowed to increase without checks, and in the last-mentioned place has rendered himself a decided nuisance by his aggressive habits towards domestic birds, for he will turn out pigeons without compunction; and the disappearance of the pretty little white Mynah (*Sturnia andamanensis*) from Ross Island in the Andamans is doubtless due to his presence there, though it is found on other islands and is sometimes brought for sale to Calcutta. The Mynah has also wild relatives here, notably the Bank Mynah (*Acridotheres ginginianus*) with its grey body colour and buff facings, set off by a red face and orange legs and bill, and the Jungle Mynah (*Aethiopsar fuscus*) which has the grey body and orange bill and legs of the bank species with the white wing and tail marks of the common one and differs from them both in being feathered up to the eyes. One naturally does not expect a simple jungle-bird to be so bare-faced as a denizen of cities. Much commoner is the sweet-voiced black and white pied Mynah (*Sturnopastor contra*) with its orange face and orange ivory-tipped bill, which is much the most like our starling, but unlike starlings generally builds a great untidy nest on a bough, as if to show that it fears no enemy; and it certainly ought not to find one in man, for its showy plumage, beautiful note, and harmless disposition, make it one of the best of our birds.

IX.—THE DHYAL.

A! Robyn, joly Robyn!—Old Ballad.

A "Robyn," as our ancestors called him, seems strange at first in black and white instead of russet and red; but half-an-hour's acquaintance with our Dhyal (*Copsychus saularis*) will show that his English name of Magpie-robin was well bestowed. Nevertheless, this name has not gained much ground in England, where the Dhyal is occasionally seen as a cage-bird—a rare and much-prized one, it is true—and has even been bred in captivity. Here he is not very commonly held in durance vile; chiefly, I suspect, because of the deservedly greater popularity of his gifted kinsman, the Shama (*Cittocincla macrura*). This is just as well, for thus more Dhyals are left to grace our gardens with their beauty and song. For the Dhyal is an exceptionally pretty bird; he is just of a nice size—intermediate between the English robin and blackbird; his pied plumage is striking, yet tasteful; and his movements are particularly graceful and animated. His mate also, although not exactly resembling him like the home Cock Robin's wife, is nevertheless very nearly as pretty, merely showing iron-grey in her plumage instead of black. She is much more retiring in her habits, and thus one sees many more cock Dhyals than hens; though, of course, it is also possible that the hens are actually less numerous as well as less obtrusive. The Dhyal can never be very abundant, for, being a purely insect-eating bird of no great travelling proclivities, he has to keep a hunting-ground to himself, and hence cannot afford to be sociable. Thus, although he is one of our commonest birds, his kind are merely found scattered about singly or in pairs; and as with so many pugnacious birds, even the two sexes do not seem to be very warmly attached, and are hardly ever close together, even though they may inhabit the same garden in peace. They need never leave it, for they are not particular about nesting accommodation, building in any hole in tree or wall. The eggs vary much in size and colour, but generally speaking resemble more or less those of the English blackbird on a small scale. And in connection with this, it is interesting to note the resemblance in proportions, gait and gestures between these birds; the two species show admirably that the names "Thrush" and "Robin" like "Duck" and "Teal," are largely only measures of size. If the Dhyal were as big as the blackbird, everyone would call it a thrush, but, as it is a good deal smaller, it gets the other name. Young Dhyals show their relationship to the thrushes by being marked with buff on the breast and wings, though generally speaking their plumage resembles that of their mother. They seem to be not difficult to rear and make nice pets. The old Dhyal is said to be very hard to tame, in spite of its confiding habits in a wild state; but my friend Mr. F. Groser has not only tamed a wild-caught old bird, but bred from him in confinement. Of course the great point is to supply abundance of insect food, and this is not difficult in

Calcutta, where shamas are so much kept that men make a trade of breeding maggots and catching grass-hoppers for their daily supply. At the same time, breeding the Dhyal is distinctly a feather in any amateur's cap, while it also shows that the bird itself is ready to accept fresh conditions. In a wild state it ranges, indeed, over a very large territory, including all the Indian Empire. It is, however, more especially a plains bird, although it ascends the Himalayas up to about 5,000 feet. At its eastern limits in South Tenasserim the black in the wings and tail begins to increase at the expense of the white, but not in places where it is noticeable on a casual view.

Nowhere have I seen the Dhyal so common as in Ross Island in the Andamans, where in the morning the air is full of the music of these birds, and they are to be seen everywhere and are particularly tame. I really don't know what they all live upon, for insects were not at all plentiful as far as I could see when I was there.

I have not noticed the Dhyal's music in Calcutta, but he does not get much chance there with the noise constantly kept up by the kites and crows. But he is certainly one of the birds which give the lie to the oft-repeated assertion that Indian birds have no song. Another is his cousin, the shama above mentioned, which is probably more numerous in cages than the Dhyal is in the wild state. The shama is a smaller bird than the Dhyal, but has a longer black and white tail and a bright chestnut stomach, so that he shows three colours. He has a voice of great power and much variety of note, and is far superior to any European singing bird except the nightingale. As he thrives so well in confinement, he has long been popular in India, and a good many are now even sent home annually. The shama is not found wild near Calcutta, and would not come into the town if he were, being, like the nightingale, rather a woodland than a garden bird; but being so nearly related to our pied songster, and so familiar a captive to boot, it is hardly possible to leave him out of consideration.

But a bird closely related to the true European robin occurs in a wild state as well as the Dhyal, and thus deserves mention. This is the Red-breasted Flycatcher (*Siphia albicilla*) a winter visitant. When he comes to us his red breast is wanting or not much in evidence, but except for this he is very like the English favourite, except that he has longer wings and shorter legs, shows some white on the tail, and is smaller altogether. This sounds as if the resemblance were not very close, but the general attitude and style of the bird make it so. As a matter of fact, flycatchers and robins are very near relatives indeed; the red-breasted flycatcher being one of the links between the two, and still retaining the habit of his robin relatives of frequently coming to the ground, which the more thorough-paced flycatchers have discarded. The real home of our little bird is in North-East Asia, for he leaves us as the hot weather comes in, like so many other birds both great and small. So although he has just as much right to the title of robin as the Dhyal, so far as appearances go, his absenteeism during most of the year may fairly bar his claim.

As for the Dhyal, he is such a nice bird in every way that I think some attempts should be made to encourage him to increase and multiply to a greater extent. Suitable house accommodation in the shape of large joints of bamboo put up near his usual haunts and in places inaccessible to enemies, and a few cockroaches or crickets put out where he can easily catch them, would probably make him very ready to enter into friendly relations with the giver of such kind assistance, and then we should have a better chance of appreciating his good qualities than is afforded us at present.

X.—THE SPARROW.

"*Look now to little Philip Sparrow.*"—*Old Ballad.*

WHY NOT? Philip himself would certainly say. Once he must have been considered a friend of man, for his nickname, derived doubtless from his note, is the earliest known to have been given to any bird, though now not in use, while Tom Tit, Mag Pie, and Jack Daw have been allowed to retain theirs; to say nothing of the redbreast, whose real name has been quite dropped in favour of his pet name of "Robin." But Philip has brought his unpopularity on himself; no doubt in England in the old days when crows and kites and other enemies, then more numerous, exercised on him the wholesome influence that they do in India, he was not sufficiently numerous to be a nuisance, and so from his familiar habits was looked on rather with a kindly eye. Of course I don't mean to imply that crows and kites keep Sparrows down by catching and eating old ones; the sublime indifference of the Sparrow in their presence is sufficient proof of the contrary. But they exercise a rigid supervision over all young birds. I remember actually seeing once a young Sparrow met on its entrance into the outside world on my verandah by three crows, who no doubt succeeded in helping it to a speedy exit; moreover, the crow prevents the sparrow from making those huge untidy nests in trees in which h s soul delights at home; in India he has to stick rigidly to holes in buildings if he wants to be safe. It is only due to Philip to say that he is a most affectionate father, and will do his utmost to warn his young of danger, flying with it and chattering in the most impressive way when its safety is threatened; and I have been reproached for days by a cock-sparrow whose offspring I had destroyed. For I think it a wise proceeding to kill, on principle, every Sparrow I can get hold of, and to encourage others to do the same. There can be no doubt that whatever his function in the world in primitive times, Philip has now outlived his usefulness, and that to a very great extent. No bird is such a thorough and unmitigated pest; field and garden produce suffers terribly from his attacks, and the insect diet he provides for his young cannot fairly be taken as a set-off for this, especially when it is considered that in his absence such insects would be taken by better birds than he, which would not levy toll on the crops as well. And the Sparrow is only too well-known as an enemy of all other birds which he can induce to vacate his vicinity by single or combined attack, or, if violence fails, by persistent mobbing and vocal annoyance. In India and in Europe, where he is a native, we do not see much of this, for he and his various feathered associates have had ages in which to settle matters and "shake down" together; but in North America, where he was introduced half a century ago, his unpleasant peculiarities have been only too evident, and the native birds have been forced to retire from the vicinity of human habitations in almost every case; while even in the old world, his hostility to our traditional allies, the beautiful and harmless swallow tribe, is still only too evident, and would of itself be a sufficient reason for his execution.

Of course it will be said that even Sparrows have their use in the economy of nature and should not be thoughtlessly wiped out; but there is no more probability of actually extirpating Philip than of arriving at the same consummation in the case of rats and mice, creatures of similar tendencies in the way of uninvited domesticity. And the work of Sparrows, whatever it may be, is equally well performed by the Tree Sparrow (*Passer montanus*), a prettier bird than *Passer domesticus*, as anyone may observe at Darjeeling, where, as in Japan and in some other parts of the world, the Tree Sparrow is the house-frequenting species. It can easily be distinguished from the house-sparrow by the fact that both male and female are like the male domestic bird, though slightly smaller and having a chocolate crown instead of a grey one, to say nothing of some minor points of difference. This bird is evidently a mountaineer and forester on account of eligible city sites being barred to it in so many places by its stronger relative; for when, as happened in one case, both were introduced together into the United States, it was found that *Passer domesticus* soon crowded out his weaker relative, which besides being smaller is much less pugnacious, and not given to annoying other birds; likewise being a less free breeder, its capacities for mischievous increase are far more limited, not the least item in "Philip's" objectionableness being his appalling powers of propagation. Were he, indeed, a less prolific bird no one would have a word to say against him, for in many respects he is deserving of the greatest admiration. Seen, as we see him in India, unsoiled by English town smoke, he is really a pretty bird in his way—a fact of which one might think him to be fully conscious, judging from the persistency with which he displays his charms before his plainly-attired spouse, who is just as likely as not to peck him for his pains. No doubt he deserves it, for he does not seem to be addicted to those gentlemanly attentions of combing his wife's hair and offering her titbits which are favoured by better-bred birds, although an ardent admirer of the sex, which generally seems to be *teterrima causa belli* with his race. And courage is certainly another good quality to be put down to Philip's credit. Alike in a single-hand fight, and in backing up a friend, he will give a good account of himself, while the same dogged tenacity has won the reluctant admiration of his unwilling American hosts when displayed in his unremitting care of his young, which he will do his best to start in the world at all costs even when handicapped by the loss of a partner, or by the unseasonable accident of a young hopeful having fallen out of the nest when too unfledged to be got back to it; other birds in such a case would often give up such a child as deserving its fate, but the despised Sparrow will stick to him and pull him through. Then again, Philip is a practical philosopher; although, unlike most finches, he has no song, he is always cheerful; one of the most versatile of birds, he will eat anything, wallow in sand or wash in water, nest anywhere, and stand any climate; for, as anyone can see, he bears the Indian heat as well as most other birds, while in the States it seems that his high northern range is limited, not so much by direct effect of cold itself as by the circumstance that it freezes the horse-droppings, on which city Sparrows depend for food to so large an extent. Nor are cities a necessity for his existence; in New Zealand, where he is now the commonest bird, he has pushed his way into the wilds, and thrives far away from civilization, having even learnt to burrow nest-holes like a sand-martin in some cases. Neither New Zealand nor Australia, however, regard him as a desirable colonist, and in fact it is his long tale of virtues and his strong and independent character which make him so objectionable. His readiness to be accommodated with food and lodging make him an economic pest and an obtrusive co-tenant of our roofs; his courage degenerates constantly into vulgar bullying, while such philoprogenitiveness as his would probably in course of time make any, even the mildest mannered and least obtrusive, bird into a nuisance. It is the fact that insect-eating birds cannot, however prolific, increase beyond a certain limit obviously imposed by their food, that makes it reasonable to recommend the continual suppression of Philip to give them more scope.

XI.—THE HONEYSUCKER.

"*For he on honey-dew hath fed.*"—*Coleridge.*

A DIET of sweets appears to have a marked effect on the bird constitution, marvellously invigorating the same instead of enervating it as one might expect. It would be difficult to find a livelier little bird than our common yellow-bellied or Amethyst-rumped Honeysucker (*Arachnechthra zeylonica*), or one more fearless and energetic. With his yellow waistcoat set off by a red velvet coat and green satin cap, he is the gayest of all our birds in dress, and as he is very tame you can get near enough to appreciate his beauty. His little olive-green mate, who keeps only the yellow vest of all her husband's brilliant attire, is usually with him, and together they merrily take their meals, of insects with sweet sauce, from the flowers, flirting their wings up and down as they hop about. For, unlike the true humming-birds of the New World, with which they are so often confounded, the Honeysuckers or Sun-birds do not feed on the wing, unless quite exceptionally, but skip from twig to twig like other little birds. At the same time they are strong and bold flyers for such tiny creatures, and although they have the bounding flight common to most small fry in feathers, will fearlessly mount high in the air and go off for a distant point as readily as a mynah or a crow. Like other honey-feeding birds, they are remarkable for courage ; I have heard of one which was long kept successfully in an aviary, and asserted his authority therein over a number of inmates larger than himself. And I myself have seen a weakly bird, which had been seized by a Brown Shrike (*Lanius cristatus*), defend himself bravely against his ruffianly adversary, though whether he escaped altogether I cannot say.

It is very probable that the reason for the courage and activity of honey-feeders lies in their mode of life ; they must be very active to obtain a sufficient quantity of their comparatively innutritious food, whether they do so by hovering bee-like like the American " hummers," or by perching and clinging on slender twigs, like our birds and the much larger Australian honey-birds. And in addition they need a long-pointed bill to run into the flowers, which in case of need becomes a bayonet-like weapon against any other bird. Our little Honeysucker's tongue is also long, and split into filaments at the tip and tubular in form, so as to suck up the liquid nectar. So fond is he of sweets, and so fearless, that a captured bird will readily sip up syrup if he be held in the hand and his bill dipped into the liquid. Indeed, for a short time the Honeysucker will appear contented enough in confinement, and continually give out his lively little song of " Chi-chit, chit-che-wee," as if he were at liberty. But unless he be provided with insect-food in addition to honey, he will not survive very long, for his dinner must include a course of meat as well as sweets. And in any case, I hope none of my readers will cage this dear little bird unless for purposes of export to Europe or elsewhere, for so harmless and happy a little being should be left alone in his native country as much as possible; though it is, I think, quite legitimate to cage such birds in order to give people who cannot see them wild some idea of what they are like in life.

When the Honeysucker's fancy lightly turns to thoughts of love, the pair construct a very curious little nest of cobwebs and rubbish, oval in shape, with the entrance-hole at the side surmounted by an eave or porch. This is hung at the end of a twig, sometimes quite low down; I remember one in the Bengal Club compound which could have been reached with the hand. On account of the nature of the materials of which it is made it does not particularly strike the eye as a nest at all, and no doubt its situation at the end of such an exiguous support serves as a protection against enemies if it does happen to draw their attention. Only two eggs are laid, white speckled with drab; and the young male birds are at first very like their mother. I knew of two being reared by hand in Calcutta by a very painstaking fancier, who kept them successfully till they had attained their full beauty of plumage, and for some time after that.

This species of Honeysucker is confined to India and Ceylon, and is certainly much the commonest kind in Calcutta. But it has a relative in India which is also frequently to be seen, and is to my mind even a handsomer bird, though less varied in hues. This is the Purple Honeysucker (*Arachnechthra asiatica*), a bird of about the same size as that which I have been discussing, but with a proportionately bigger bill, both longer and stouter, although maintaining the curved and slender form so characteristic of these birds.

The male of this species is clad throughout in rich metallic purple, set off by a flame-coloured tuft under each armpit which is ordinarily concealed by the wings. It projects, however, when the bird is settled for repose, and is, I believe, shown off in courtship.

The hen is olive and yellow like that of the yellow-bellied species, but she can easily be distinguished by her bigger bill, and by having a yellow throat as well as breast; the throat in the hen of the commoner bird being of a dirty white, not yellow. The Purple cock apparently thinks his wedding garment too expensive to be worn the whole year round; for after nesting he doffs it, and assumes female plumage, retaining only a purple streak from chin to stomach as a mark of his sex. The young cocks are at first like the hen, not having even this distinctive mark.

This species of Honeysucker is a quieter and less sociable bird than the other; he is commonly seen alone, has a great fancy for particular spots, and does not flirt his wings like his rival. He is, however, a much better songster, being nearly equal to a canary; and sings much merely to amuse himself. I well remember one bird which came to the Museum compound after breeding to change his plumage; he kept very much to two or three trees, singing, apparently, from one particular twig, and even when in undress he kept up his song. The Purple Honeysucker has a much wider range than the other, being found from Persia to Cochin China, and it also ascends further up the hills. It is, therefore, evidently, a more hardy and adaptable bird; and as its ordinary feeding and nesting-habits are the same as those of the other species,

I do not quite understand why it is not so common in Calcutta. Very probably, however, its more lively relative's competition is too much for it there. I certainly noticed that one bird, which I took alive to the London Zoo some years ago, seemed afraid of the yellow-bellied birds confined with him, all of which succumbed on the journey—the last one distinctly bullying his dark companion. Other people have since repeated my experiment with the purple kind, and I believe this would thrive in the open in Southern Europe if turned out there; a more charming ornament to a garden it would be difficult to find.

Gold-backed Woodpecker.
(*Brachypternus aurantius.*)

XII.—THE WOODPECKER.

"*The golden woodpecker...... laughs loud at nothing.*"
—*Hurdis.*

It would appear that a propensity for irresponsible and irrelevant hilarity is widely spread in the Woodpecker family; for the species alluded to by the worthy author of the "Village Curate" is the English Green Woodpecker (*Gecinus viridis*)—a bird which can hardly even by a stretch of the poetical imagination be called golden, by the way. Our own common Calcutta Woodpecker (*Brachypternus aurantius*) is just as unseasonably jovial. He is jolliest when on the wing; if you watch after hearing his ringing cackle, you will generally be rewarded by a sight of his somewhat ungainly form, as, with head outstretched and legs drawn up, he progresses with his curious flight—first a flutter and then a dip with closed wings—to some tree-trunks which he intends to explore. He is not shy, and will readily permit you to admire his old-gold back and scarlet crest as he hitches himself up the bark, sounding for insects as he goes. His motto is ever *excelsior*, for Woodpeckers always work upwards, though they can slip down backwards or laterally round the trunk of their tree if they wish. The foot of the Woodpecker, with the toes in pairs, is supposed to be especially fitted for this kind of travelling. But this is open to doubt; some other birds which do not climb, like the woodpeckers, near relatives the barbets, have the same arrangement; and if it be so convenient for a climbing bird to have two toes behind instead of one, why are the woodpeckers as a family gradually getting rid of the inner hind toe? This is always smaller than the outer one, and not unfrequently absent altogether; while in some species, as in the Golden-backed one under discussion, the toe is there indeed, but in the form of a tiny useless vestige that has to be looked for carefully.

There are other points in our feathered carpenter's structure, however, about the usefulness of which no doubt can exist. His stiff wiry tail, which is never cocked up as it is by other birds, is a most admirable prop to support him as he clings vertically to the tree, and his hard chisel-tipped beak contains a most curious tongue, long and worm-like, and armed with a many-barbed horny tip. This he can shoot out with great facility to some distance, as its base is supported by a pair of bony springs; and altogether it is an admirable instrument for exploring crevices and persuading any grub which may lie hid therein to come out to dinner.

It is also useful in enabling the bird to lick up the juice of soft fruit, though whether this forms part of his diet in a wild state I cannot say. Probably it does, as it seems very acceptable in captivity, a condition to which this species is readily reconciled—at any rate if taken young. A young Woodpecker, indeed, makes a very interesting pet in several ways. Like a young barbet, it possesses a warty pad on the hocks, and shuffles about thereon for some time, not getting really on to its feet till it is full-fledged. It is not till then, too, that the curious arrow tip of the tongue is fully developed—this being at first devoid of barbs. The first plumage, however, which springs from a skin unclothed by any baby-garment of down, is just as bright as that of the old birds, and indicates the sex of its wearer at once—a very rare case among birds. For the young hen Woodpecker has her forehead black, sometimes speckled with white like her mother's, while in father and son the red of the crest runs forward right up to the beak. How young Woodpeckers get on in their close quarters in a hole hewed out by the parents I don't know, but their tempers must suffer considerably by enforced restraint, for I have seen brother and sister fight savagely in captivity while still fledglings. Nor do the birds seem at all sociable in their habits when wild; indeed, one does not usually see even a pair together. Business is business, and a hard-working bird like a Woodpecker has no time to spare for social amenities.

Laborious as the lives of Woodpeckers seem to be, however, they are a thriving clan, and are spread all over the world except in the Australian region, from the icy pine-forests of the Arctic regions to the warm damp jungles of South America.

The Golden-backed Woodpecker has not so wide a range as some other species, but it is still a very numerous bird, being found all over India except in the higher hills. It varies to a certain extent with locality, like so many other Indian birds, Sind specimens being paler and South Indian ones darker than the type found in Calcutta. There is a certain amount of individual variation also; the black-and-white waistcoat of some birds is darker than that of others, and the golden mantle may show a strong tinge of red. In fact, if extreme forms be taken, two or three species can be made out of our present subject.

It is more interesting, however, to note that the plumage of this species is very nearly reproduced by two others, one of which (*Chrysocolaptes gutticristatus*) has a well-developed inner hind-toe, while the other (*Tiga javanensis*) has none at all; so that the common Golden-backed Woodpecker forms the middle term in this series of degenerates, and is a fine example of a "missing link" still existing, to use a rather Hibernian expression. It is very remarkable, indeed, that Woodpeckers should be so undecided in the matter of toes; as I implied above, the reason is not easy to find, as generally speaking they are so very uniform in structure and habits. All agree in laying white eggs, and in refusing to wear any shade of blue in their plumage, and most are inveterate woodlanders; for the

Ground Woodpecker (*Colaptes campestris*) of the South American Pampas has gladly turned his attention to trees now that they have been planted on his native plains. In fact, his enthusiastic carpentering performed on the as yet none too luxuriant plantations has rendered him rather an economic pest, unlike the majority of the family. For Woodpeckers are, generally speaking, among the most useful of birds, attacking the destructive woodboring insects which few other species can reach, and serving as a wholesome check on the industrious ant, which in the East finds so many ways of exercising its ingenuity to our discomfort.

XIII.—THE COPPERSMITH.

"*Only the song of a secret bird.*"—*Swinburne.*

Vox et prœterea nihil, indeed, is *Xantholœma hœmatocephala* to most of us; for though many, vexed by his monotonous music through the blazing weather in which he delights, may have exclaimed with the apostle "Alexander the Coppersmith hath wrought me much evil," few have seen him face to face. Nor can one reasonably be expected to see a pudgy little green bird, not much bigger than a sparrow, with distinct ventriloquial proclivities, and an aspiring spirit which leads him to prefer tall trees to bushes. Nevertheless, Alexander sometimes descends lower, and then one may see and admire his coral feet and crimson and primrose head-marking, and realize that a bird which would be striking in any country is really one of our commonest citizens, for when once you know him by sight you may see him almost anywhere, even in the trees in the streets; while long before his personal acquaintance is made his continual "tonk-tonk-tonk," repeated indefinitely like the tick of grandfather's clock, attests his ubiquity. Even in the cold weather he will tune up at times, but he does not really do himself justice till it gets warm, though he feels the heat as much as other birds, for I have caught him gasping for breath like any crow. No doubt, as he is an energetic little bird, he is often scant of breath, for like all the barbet family, to which he belongs, he is of a somewhat clumsy build, and not adapted for active exercise in a warm climate. Nevertheless he thrives exceedingly; his food, of wild fruits, is abundant, and he can peck out a home in any old tree; barbets, like woodpeckers, excavating their own quarters, and nobly despising any luxury in the form of bedding within. Both barbets and woodpeckers have the toes in pairs like a parrot's, two in front and two behind, which as stated above, has been cited in the case of the latter birds as a beautiful adaptation for climbing; but as nuthatches climb better than woodpeckers with toes of the ordinary three-to-one arrangement, and as barbets don't climb at all, but just hop, that theory is insufficient.

One very puzzling point about the Coppersmith is his whiskers. His stout black bill is garnished with a sort of straggly moustache of the "cricketer" type—eleven a side—which does not appear to be either ornamental or useful. Both sexes have it, the female Coppersmith being in all respects like her mate, and it is common to many other barbets, but not to all; though such whiskers crop up again in other birds of quite different families. These are generally insect-eaters, but some barbets which do eat insects are clean-shaven ones, so no connection with that habit will account for Alexander's hirsuteness. In fact the use of the "rictal bristles," as ornithologists call such appendages, is one of the puzzles presented by birds which have not as yet been solved. Young barbets, like young woodpeckers do not move about on their toes, but on their heels, and they have a similar hard heel-pad to protect the joint and give them a grip; when they are fledged and hop about it gradually disappears. Another curious trick of Alexander's family is their ingenious custom of turning their tails over their backs, beneath the wings, when pigging together in their very limited quarters, obviously to economise space. They never quite get out of the habit, for though a barbet most steadily keeps his tail pointed down in the daytime, at night he forgets himself and the unruly appendage makes a wild attempt to turn over as in childhood's days, but cannot get further than an angle of forty-five degrees. The big Himalayan Barbet (*Megalæma marshallorum*), however, has mastered the difficulty, and can keep his tail properly drooping like any ordinary birds. To return to the little Coppersmiths; they emerge from white eggs, and are presumably quite nude at first, though I have never seen any so young; when they fledge off they show no red colour anywhere, being merely green with yellow faces and flesh-coloured feet. They are extremely easy to rear on plantain cut up and administered with a quill, and very readily learn to peck for themselves as soon as fledged. It is very curious indeed, that the dealers have never taken them up as they have the larger Blue-cheeked Barbet (*Cyanops asiatica*), of which more anon. The fact is, that the Coppersmith, although he will eat it, cannot live on the universal pea-meal paste, but will die in a few days if allowed to devour the unwholesome mess. But give him his natural fruit diet, and he will live well, even if caught wild; and hand-reared birds, at all events, will thrive on bread-and-milk also. I knew one such which could not ultimately be distinguished in beauty of plumage from a wild bird, though on its first assumption of the adult plumage it was less brilliant. This bird's brother distinguished himself by a very intelligent performance. He watched his opportunity and darted out when the door of the aviary was opened, but returned in a day or so, to stay contented for a short time and then repeat his sudden exit, this time never to return. It looked as if he were taking his bearings and learning how to get a living before he made up his mind to go off altogether. The Coppersmith seems to make an intelligent and interesting pet if hand-reared, but he is not sociable with other birds, though not aggressive. But, like Hannibal Chollop, he requires a clear space round him, and if he be crowded either with his own species or with other birds, there will be trouble, for barbets are hard bitten birds and tenacious of what they conceive to be their rights; indeed a couple of wild Coppersmiths have been seen to fight till one was quite worn out. Steady persistence, in fact, seems to be the key-note of a barbet's character, whether it be calling, eating, or fighting: the young birds start practising their note before they are fledged, and everyone knows with what relentless persistency the old bird keeps up his banging on imaginary metal. At his meals, too, the Coppersmith is quietly energetic, eating a very large quantity for his size, as indeed, he needs to do, his diet seeming to be very imperfectly assimilated, as is the case with many other fruit-eating birds. A curious fact about the Coppersmith is his liability to albinism, or rather lutinism, for the pale forms of green birds are yellow, not white. A beautiful specimen of a lutino Coppersmith was, when this book was written, in the Calcutta Zoo, and was interesting in that the red on the plumage and legs persisted, although the bill was fleshy white, and only a little of the green feathering was to be seen, in the wings and tail mostly. Of course even if these pallid birds could hold their own with the normally coloured ones, they would still be at a disadvantage in the struggle for existence, since their colour would be no protection; but the red on the present bird showed that it

Blue-cheeked Barbet.
(*Cyanops asiatica.*

had moulted at least once, and so managed to exist for a year at all events. The Coppersmith must, however, be a singularly successful species, for it is not only very common but has a wide range east of India to the Philippines. In this respect it has the advantage of our other Calcutta species, the Blue-cheeked Barbet above mentioned, a very showy bird as large as a thrush, with sky-blue in place of primrose-yellow on the cheeks and throat. This bird is less common in Calcutta than the Coppersmith, and is confined to India and Burma, though it ranges higher up the hills than the small species. It is blessed with a better digestion and temper than Alexander, and will assimilate pea-meal brose successfully and stand crowding; and so it gets frequently caged and sent to Europe. In fact a very tame bird of this kind, which lived for years at the London Zoo, was the first barbet I ever saw alive, and every now and then it turns up in a dealer's shop or a bird show. It is true that its "song of colour" pitched as it is in brilliant red, blue, and green, rises to a shriek, and that its triple call of "*kuturruk*" is about three times as monotonous as Alexander's foundry-work, so that its popularity as a cage bird is never likely to be wide. Nevertheless I must confess to a great liking for barbets; their form, if not beautiful, is quaint, and their colouring gorgeous, if a little barbaric. And as to the noise they make, it is at least constant and consistent, and has not the exasperating quality of intermittence which is so annoying in some feathered vocalists, the domestic fowl for instance. The sturdy smith has always been a popular character, and I hope such may always be the case with his fellow artisan in feathers.

XIV.—THE BLUE-JAY.

"*A lovely bird, with azure wings.*"—*Byron.*

ONE can hardly go on with the above quotation and credit the subject of the present article with a "song that said a thousand things," for the Blue-jay's vocalizations are limited to a degree. Ordinarily, as has been neatly remarked, he "encourages himself in patience" by uttering a sound like "tschok" at intervals, and more rarely he points his bill to heaven and his tail to earth and utters a cackling laugh, in feeble imitation of the great Australian kingfisher, commonly known as the Laughing Jackass (*Dacalo gigas*). As a matter of fact, our present friend is more kingfisher than jay, this poverty of vocabulary being one of the points in which the relationship comes out; real jays having a remarkable flexibility of voice, though their ordinary remarks are not much more musical than those of the Roller family, to which the Indian Blue-jay really belongs. Rollers also agree with kingfishers and differ from jays in several easily noticeable points of habit, to say nothing of more recondite anatomical distinctions. Thus, they extend their feet behind when flying, instead of drawing them up to the breast like the crow tribe; they bolt their food whole, never tearing it with bill and foot like the real jay; they are practically pure animal feeders, and do not lay up stores against a time of scarcity, unlike the omnivorous and, provident corvine jays; and most important of all, they nest in holes and lay white eggs. It is this common confusion between two groups of birds very well known in their respective habitats that makes it excusable to include in this series a bird which is not common in Calcutta by any means. In fact, I was personally acquainted with only one wild specimen, who was generally to be seen on one of the furlong posts of the race-course, just opposite the jail. Hereabouts he spent most of his time, for Rollers, again unlike the birds whose name they borrow, are very sedentary birds, waiting till they see some small live thing and then pouncing upon it, instead of actively hunting about. As to the quality of the game they are not very particular, for, as I have proved with a captive bird, they will eat and digest toads, which are a good deal too much for some birds' insides. The Roller throws up the hard parts of its food in quids or pellets, like many other insectivorous birds. Young Rollers are ugly little creatures at first, being quite naked, but when the feathers have grown enough to cover the body they are very pretty, their plumage, with the wings and tail banded with Oxford and Cambridge blue, being like that of their parents ; for, unlike many brilliant birds, the Indian Roller has a common livery for all ages and both sexes. The large dark eyes also do not change with age, and give the young birds a singularly innocent appearance, which rather belies their real disposition; for they are greedy little creatures, and when hungry will fight violently over their food; although I have seen a youngster which I had filled up kindly present an extra piece to a brother fledgling. Young Rollers are quite easy to rear if fed on raw meat and cockroaches, and will grow up very tame. But they are not interesting pets, for in a small cage they beat and break their beautiful plumage, and in an aviary sit still so much that they are not a very great acquisition. Indeed, so sedentary are the Roller's ordinary habits, and so inconspicuous are the pinky drab and sea-green of his plumage in repose, that our American winter visitors have called him "the surprise bird," in allusion to the startling display of colour he gives as he takes wing, looking like a great butterfly in his lazy flapping flight. Like many of these weak-looking fliers, however, he is really very active in the air, as might have been seen in the case of the race-course habitué abovementioned when he was badgered by the local crows, who seemed to cherish a prejudice against him.

The *Nilkant*, as the Roller is called by the natives, is with them a sacred bird, and once at least a throne has been gained by the holy fowl—no doubt a trained specimen—alighting on the successful candidate's head. And certainly if beauty deserves the honour of worship, the Roller has full right to it, more especially as he is absolutely harmless; for, when he does fly, he is almost the most effective bird one could have in a landscape. Fortunately, although I fear many have been killed for their plumage, the Roller is, over a large part of this country, exceedingly common, and extends westwards through Persia to the Levant. Hereabouts he is on the confines of his eastern range, for from about the longitude of Calcutta he begins to intermarry with the darker Burmese species, called by naturalists *Coracias affinis*, our bird being *Cora-*

cias indica. The Burmese bird is rather larger than ours and very much darker in the general tone of its plumage, although curiously enough the tail is lighter, not having the purple band at the tip which so well sets off that of the Indian bird. The young, also, of the Burmese Roller are different from the parents, being much lighter and duller. This species must be found wild near Calcutta, though I have never seen it even on the telegraph wires by the railway; but I have seen some more or less pure Burmese specimens brought in, fresh-caught, for sale, and have successfully "meated them off," as bird-fanciers say, together with the common bird. For it is easy enough to get adult Rollers to feed in confinement if you start them on cockroaches all—more or less—alive and kicking. Water they do not constantly require, for they seldom appear to drink when they have the chance, in this total abstinence again resembling the kingfishers; but unlike those birds they not only bathe, but wallow and shuffle in dust like a fowl when they want a clean-up.

It is curious that, being so easy to keep in confinement, the Indian Roller has so seldom been sent to England. Some time ago a well-known London fancier of birds obtained a very seedy specimen from a dealer, and more recently my friend Mr. E. W. Harper of this city succeeded in sending one to the London Zoo, where it is still in good health. The curious thing was that, though tame enough in Calcutta, the bird became for a time very wild and nervous in London. But the very intelligent keeper who had it in charge told me that he had found the European Rollers, which he had had for some time in his care, also very timid, and the same thing was noted about this latter species (*Coracias garrula*) by Bechstein in his work on cage birds more than a century ago; so that possibly the peculiarity runs in the family. The European Roller, which also occurs in the extreme north-west of India, and comes to England frequently to get shot and "recorded," is a migratory species, with much more pale blue and less purple in its plumage than our "Blue-jay." Curiously enough, it is sometimes called in German the Birch-jay, so that the superficial resemblance to the jay has struck Europeans independently in two distant countries.

The Americans, however, do not seem to have been taken in, being no doubt too well acquainted with their own Blue-jay (*Cyanocitta cristata*), which really is in a literal sense what its name proclaims it to be. There are no Rollers in America, and when Brother Jonathan gets over the unreasonable horror of acclimatization with which his too successful experiment with Philip Sparrow has filled him, he cannot do better than set to work to supply the deficiency with a big consignment of our lovely Indian species; for the Roller would not only be a great ornament to the prairies, but a very useful ally in grass-hopper plagues.

White-breasted Kingfisher.
(*Halcyon smyrnensis.*)

XV.—THE KINGFISHER.

"*On the shore*
The halcyons loved of Thetis spread their wings."—
Virgil.

THERE seems to be some reason for suspecting that the goddess's pets were terns, not Kingfishers after all; but nevertheless Aristotle describes a bird as at any rate one sort of "halcyon" which certainly could not have been anything else but a Kingfisher. Moreover, in various parts of its wide range across the Old World the Kingfisher often finds itself on the shore and takes kindly enough to a diet of salt-water fish and shrimps. But it is by rights a haunter of trees overhanging fresh water; its little coral feet, with the front toes joined together by skin, are better suited for perching than for walking, and all it ever does in the way of pedestrianism is a very short waddle.

As it is not adapted for hopping about the twigs either, and furthermore has not very long wings, it wisely sits still on whatever point of vantage presents itself, and thence plunges on its prey with a determined splash. If there is no suitable perch, it will fly up and hover for a short time, but this more laborious procedure it naturally does not adopt if it can be avoided. Our little Indian Kingfisher has sometimes been ranked as a distinct species from the home bird (*Alcedo ispida*) and called *Alcedo bengalensis*; but it really does not deserve such distinction, being simply a rather undersized variety. That this should be so is curious; the Kingfishers are essentially a tropical family, pushing out here and there hardy pioneers into colder climates. And yet here we find that the European bird, which too often starves to death when winter lock up the fresh waters it frequents, nevertheless has a finer physique than when living in its native tropics, where food is almost always plentiful. In another way the Kingfisher is better off in the East, in that it is not much persecuted by man, although even here far too many are killed for their feathers. But it is not relentlessly hunted down here as it is in England; presumably because bright birds are more numerous and destructive fools with guns less so. So our little halcyon is as tame as a robin, and all the details of his daily life may be watched. He is a great believer in "spheres of influence," and seems to require a large tank all to himself; for if I saw another bird besides our usual resident at the Museum tank, there was apt to be an amount of tail-cocking and wing-drooping going on, which argued matrimony in prospect, and hence the tolerance of a stranger is explained. Where the burrow, in which their pinky white eggs are deposited in due season, may be, I do not know; but it is not surprising that it should be some little distance off, for Kingfishers often nest some distance away from water. The half-fledged young are funny little things, for their feathers grow to some length before bursting their sheaths, so that the resulting appearance rather suggests a miniature porcupine. Moreover, they rival the Hibernian of fiction in their ability to "advance backward," a useful accomplishment to dwellers in holes. They fledge off into a plumage not much inferior in brilliance to that of their parents, who, in their turn, each sport an azure mantle and cinnamon breast, not being addicted to invidious sexual distinctions in dress, though the hen alone shows a red streak on the bill. But brilliant as is the little Kingfisher, he is quite eclipsed by his larger relative, the White-breasted species (*Halcyon smyrnensis*). This bird is as big as a thrush and is most richly attired in sky-blue and chocolate, set off by a white shirt-front and red bill and feet. He is, in fact, quite the showiest bird we have in Calcutta, and is more in evidence generally than the small species, since he does not confine himself to water, feeding on worms, grasshoppers, &c., as well as aquatic prey. Indeed, he does not seem to be much of a fisher, for when he does strike at something in the water, he glides down slantingly and touches the surface in a very half-hearted way, although when taking his bath he dashes in boldly enough. Obtrusive as he is in colours, he is still more so in voice, and deems it necessary whenever he takes wing to let the neighbourhood know he is moving by uttering a loud unpleasant cackle. Occasionally, presumably when under the influence of the tender passion, he will fly erratically about uttering a wailing note; but his flight is not swift at any time, and very different from the arrow-like progress of his little kinsman. The two seem to get on all right together, for they frequent the same tank in peace—no doubt because their lines of business are not quite identical, as I remarked above. Although, however, he is more or less of a Jack-of-all-trades for a Kingfisher, the white-breasted bird has not nearly so wide a range as the little one, for, though found from Cyprus to China, he is essentially a bird of warm climates. His versatility is shown in his nesting-habits as well as in his feeding, for though he usually nests in a burrow like his family generally, he has been observed in Cachar to actually make a rough nest of moss among rocks—a most anomalous habit; for kingfishers, in addition to being burrowers, usually despise all bedding, and allow the family to pig together on a sort of mat of fish-bones which have been cast up in "quids" after the flesh has been digested.

In this larger Kingfisher, as in the other, male and female have the same plumage, and the young merely a rather duller one; but the beaks and feet of the youngsters are blackish instead of red. The male, when courting, makes a great display of his wings, which have a fine white patch on the primary quills, like the mynah's; while the wing-covers are quite diagrammatically coloured, the "major" being blue, the "median" black, and the "minor" chestnut—a useful "tip" for anyone who wants to learn the topography of a bird's wing according to the ornithological books. *Halcyon smyrnensis* bears captivity very well, and has been exhibited both at the London and the Calcutta Zoological Gardens.

There is a sort of larger edition of him, nearly as big as a crow, which one may see as near as Alipore; this bird rejoices in the name of *Pelargopsis gurial*, the Stork-billed Kingfisher. He is not as showy as his smaller relatives, being buff and pale-blue in colour, and has a curiously plaintive call for such a big strong bird. He is a fish feeder, although in form he resembles the White-breasted species more than the little fisher, and likewise has a red bill. I have never seen about Calcutta the pretty spotted Pied Kingfisher (*Ceryle varia*), whose plumage always reminds me of a silver-spangled Hamburgh fowl; but he is sure to be found not far off, for he is one of our commonest Indian birds, and in a slightly different form extends to Africa and Western Asia also.

Sometimes, however, one may see in Calcutta a bird which, although not a Kingfisher, is nevertheless a very near relative of that family, and therefore ought not to be entirely passed over, especially as he generally goes under an *alias*. This is the Green Bee-eater (*Merops viridis*), commonly miscalled a flycatcher. The term describes his way of getting a living well enough, but in his general form, except that he has a curved instead of a straight beak, and a long tail, he is very kingfisher-like. When in the hand, it may be observed that his feet are of the same peculiar make as those of Kingfishers, and he burrows out a nest in the same manner, and lays similar eggs. Bee-eaters are very nice little birds; they are more sociable than their relatives, and several sit about together; and they also breed in societies, making a regular warren where they are numerous. Like Philip Sparrow, also, they are among the few birds which both dust themselves and bathe, which argues an intelligent appreciation of all the simple pleasures open to a bird. When dusting they, of course, have to settle; but they take their bath by a plunge like a swallow. They are not constant residents in Calcutta—at any rate one only notices them at certain seasons, and then their pretty green plumage and graceful flight make them very conspicuous. Although one of the smallest of the family, being, except for his long tail, only about as big as a sparrow, the Green Bee-eater is a most prosperous species, extending from North-East Africa to Cochin China. As with so many wide-ranging birds, the Bee-eater's coat varies locally. In the North-West of India his throat becomes more or less blue, while in Burma he frequently sports an auburn cap. This is an example of one way in which species arise. If the pure-green strain died out on account of unfavourable conditions, the blue-throated and chestnut-headed varieties would be two distinct species. But of course this does not explain how the different varieties arose in the first place, which is the real problem of the origin of species.

XVI.—THE SWIFT.

"True to the kindred points of heaven and home."—Wordsworth.

WHAT the gentle bard sang of the English sky-lark is still more applicable to our long-winged, dusky house-fellow who squeals and skims round the constituent buildings of "The City of Palaces" much as his near relative does about English towns and villages: for house-swifts hardly ever alight outside their nests, and only go there to rest, sit, and sleep, performing all the other functions of life on the wing. The Indian Swift (*Cypselus-affinis*), indeed, is neither so loud nor so speedy as the English one (*Cypselus apus*); this, indeed, could hardly be expected of him, as he is not so large a bird; but he is certainly prettier, being greenish black instead of sooty brown, and with his dark hue set off by a patch of pure white above the tail, which is not forked as in the home bird. As in Swifts generally, there is no noticeable difference between male and female; and the young are merely duller by reason of a light fringing to their feathers. One has plenty of opportunities of studying them, as they are unusually happy at falling out of their stuffy nests, composed of all sorts of rubbish that the parents can pick up on the wing and stick together against some roof or in a crack with their gummy saliva. Glutinous salivation is indeed a speciality with the Swifts, and the celebrated birds' nests of which soup is made to gladden the hearts of such Chinese bigwigs as can afford to pay about its weight in silver for the raw material are the product of certain birds of this family who rely for their procreant cradles simply on unlimited expectoration; those which adulterate their secretion with feathers and other extraneous substances producing a far less marketable article. The eggs of this Swift, like those of its family, generally, are long and white, and few in number, only two to four being laid; the young are nasty, naked, pink little things, at first blind, with their little helpless wings no bigger than their legs; then, as the feathers sprout, the wings predominate by degrees, till in the full-grown bird the puny legs only serve to carry the strong grappling claws which the bird needs for scrambling about and hanging on in its confined nesting and roosting quarters. The toes are not placed three in front and one behind, as in most birds, but spread out anyhow like the "fingers" of a starfish, and they grip very closely. On one occasion I picked up in the Museum two birds, presumably rival males, so tightly clenched by their feet that they did not separate even when taken in hand. The Swift seems, as might be expected with such feet, not to be able to walk like other birds, but only to crawl in a shuffling flat-footed fashion like a nestling, with the hocks touching the ground; and I had to catch one and tie its wings to find this out, for if you place a Swift on the ground he wastes no time in pedestrianism on his own account, but jerks himself into the air at once —if he can, for both this species and the home Swift have been said to be incapable of rising when once down. I have, however, several times experimented with our bird and with one exception always found uninjured birds could get under way, even the two fighters I mentioned above; but I did get one specimen which apparently could not start till I threw it up in the air. It is not difficult to get hold of Swifts for experiment, for of all the birds I have met with, the Indian Swift is the best hand at getting into a scrape at any age; several times I have heard the piteous squeals of one in the grip of a crow, and I once extracted a wretched individual from a drain, too weak to fly when he was released; while getting into a room, forgetting the way out, and so circling round hopelessly till he drops is quite the ordinary thing for a Swift to do; I presume if he is driven out of his nest he is altogether lost for the time.

The Swift, indeed, does not compare at all favourably for intelligence with the swallow, whose name or nest he sometimes usurps. Into the anatomical distinctions between the two it is not my intention here to enter; but roughly Swifts may be distinguished from swallows by having only ten instead of twelve tail-feathers, or if one cannot catch them for the purpose of noting this distinction, by the Swift's habits, noticed above, of not perching away from home. The swallows sit both on dead twigs and telegraph wires, and when they have occasion to come to the ground for mud, can walk as much as they want with their pretty little feet, which are just miniatures of those of ordinary birds. But one does not often see swallows in Calcutta to make the comparison, though our common Chimney Swallow (*Hirundo rustica*) which also is found here, and breeds in the Himalayas, does turn up sometimes, especially in the cold weather. Perhaps the Swifts have had something to say in the matter, for, as I hinted above, they are rather too much for swallows when the interests of the two happen to clash, the swallow's nice mud nest being a great temptation to a dishonest Swift. However, Swifts and swallows of numerous species do exist out here together, so that probably as a rule they do not get in each other's way. The English Swift, for instance, occurs in the hills and Kashmir, and in Calcutta itself the little Palm Swift (*Tachornis batassiensis*) may be found as well as the House Swift. The Palm Swift is a considerably smaller and slenderer bird than the domestic species, with a well-forked tail and plain drab plumage all over; it is not a very rapid flyer, and keeps near the palms, on the fronds of which it fastens its tiny cup-like nest of plant-down or feather, stuck together and fastened in one of the furrows of the leaf by the usual salivary cement. There was a small colony inhabiting a tall fan-palm in the Museum compound.

Wherever the fan-palm grows in India the Palm Swift takes up its abode, but the house bird, not being so fastidious in its requirements, is at home wherever there are cliffs or buildings in Africa and India, and the intervening countries; indeed, I first made its acquaintance at Mombasa in one of the offices of the British East Africa Company nearly a dozen years ago. East of India the House-Swift is blacker and sports a longer forked tail, and so claims rank as a distinct species (*Cypselus subfurcatus*), but to go into the Swifts of the Indian region would be getting too far away from the birds of Calcutta altogether, so that I will confine myself to further stating that the little producer of the best quality of edible nests (*Collocalie francica*) breeds in the Andamans and Nicobars, though he wilfully refuses to be civilized and inhabit houses; which is the more vexatious as a near relative of his (*Collocalia linchi*), who builds a nest so adulterated with moss as to be quite worthless, has taken freely to buildings at Port Blair, and can be studied there readily. Perhaps transposing the eggs of the two species might persuade the first class bird not to waste his sweetness on the desert rocks, and they breed at the same time; so valuable a product ought to be worth a little trouble in its cultivation. As for our humble companion here, he is to be tolerated if not loved; it is difficult to get up much interest in Swifts, which have never enjoyed the popularity of swallows; but think of what we might have to put up with in the way of insects if he were not here to make at least *some* impression on their numbers! For Swifts, as every one probably knows, live on small winged insects, and of all the places in which I have ever lived, Calcutta is *facile princeps* in the production of such amenities of existence.

Hen Koël.
(*Eudynamis honorata.*)

XVII.—THE KOËL.

"*O Koël, little Koël, singing on the siris bough.*"—
Kipling.

It is in my mind, as Mr. Kipling's animal say, that our Anglo-Indian laureate has in the above-quoted passage grievously mixed up the Koël with the Coppersmith, a miscreant dealt with earlier in this series. For the Koël is not so very small as birds go, being as big as a good sized pigeon, nor, though his "speech" is "ceaseless" enough in the season of his vocalizations, is it "bell-like;" while the Coppersmith's metallic call might deserve such an epithet. I must confess to being heretical about the Koël, who is not as a rule a popular character with the exile in India whose fate Mr. Kipling so pathetically deplores. No note among our English song birds' utterances, save only the lark's or the nightingale's, is to my ear so pleasant as the "kuk, kuk, ko-eel, ko-eel, ko-eel," running up the scale, with which *Eudynamis honorata* warns us that the time to stew in our own juice is at hand. The natives, who enjoy the said culinary process, love the Koël, and deem his jetty plumage a fit object with which to compare the locks of beauty, even as European poets do the raven's. They also evince their admiration of his song by keeping him caged, and he seems to do very well in confinement, although he must find *satoo*—gram-meal paste—a somewhat monotonous diet in place of his natural fare of jungle fruits. However, the birds of the cuckoo family, to which he belongs, have accommodating stomachs, so long as the food be soft and plentiful, and the Koël especially must have a hardy constitution to withstand the load of mixed garbage with which his infant interior is presumably filled by his natural foster-parent, the crow. It is much in the Koël's favour that after such an upbringing he reverts to vegetarianism; and how he gets brought up at all under the circumstances is somewhat of a puzzle. There is no doubt whatever that crows hate the old Koëls and persecute them literally to the death when they get the chance; nevertheless, they perform a parent's duties to their offspring when once the supposititious bantling has been safely foisted into the corvine nest. To get this done the male Koël is said to show himself and draw off pursuit while his mate, who is speckled like a hen pheasant and not in the least like him, deposits her egg where it is to receive parental attention. As the said egg is very like a crow's there is no great wonder that it should be hatched as if it were one; nor can a crow be expected to notice that the changeling's toes are in pairs, not three in front and one behind, as crows' toes should properly be. But one would expect that when the young bird is fledged its appearance would provoke suspicion. It is not so big as a young crow, and though it is sometimes as black as its real or foster-father it generally betrays a certain speckling, more or less according to its sex, of the plumage of its maternal parent; though even the lightest coloured young hen Koël, by her dark bill and eyes, is easily distinguished from her mother, whose ruby eyes and jade-green bill are like those of her husband. Probably, by the time that the hen crow awakes to the fact that she has been "sold again," maternal affection—that powerful force which makes cats foster rats, and wolves babies—has asserted itself to such an extent that she cannot bid the intruder begone.

It is sometimes stated, however, that the real parent hangs about, so as to be ready in such a contingency, and certainly there seems to be some feeling of propriety among Koëls, in spite of their disreputable family connexions. I have seen the male take the trouble to feed the female with berries plucked off the tree on which both were sitting; and I am not aware that even so small an act of courtesy as this is has been recorded of the home cuckoo. It is possible therefore that care of offspring as well as attention to the conjugal tie is a little more in evidence in the Indian bird.

Both our common crows, the urban and the mofussilite, are victimized by the Koël, but the former more frequently than the latter, probably because the town crow is the smaller bird; and as a family upset by this cuculine intrusion is almost the only calamity crows have to fear from other feathered members of creation, it is a great pity the Koël is not commoner—though some people, who object to the persistence of the sable vocalizer by night as well as by day, would probably say there are far too many of his kind about already. Such have been known to confound the Koël with the brain-fever bird, which, however, is a quite distinct species, much more like the home cuckoo,

Brain-fever bird.
(*Hierococcyx varius.*)

and known in books as the Hawk-cuckoo (*Hierococcyx varius*) form his remarkable resemblance in plumage and general form and flight to the common Indian Sparrow-hawk or Shikra (*Astur badius*). His note, however, fully entitles him to his ordinary designation, whether from its "damnable iteration" or from its remarkable resemblance to the word "brain-fever" repeated in a piercing voice running up the scale; although an equally worthy rendering of the performance, which has the merit of including the overture preceding the triple note, is, "O lor'! O lor'! how very hot it's getting—I feel it, I feel it," &c., &c., &c. The brain-fever bird in youth is nurtured by the "seven sisters," and in connection with his resemblance to the shikra it may be noted that one observer states that the whole sisterhood make themselves scarce when *Hierococcyx* appears on the scene, and thus give her a fair field for planting her oval imposition on them. On the other hand, as has been stated in the chapter dealing with those birds, the shabby seven have been known to show a bold front to the real enemy, and moreover the young brain-fever bird is as similar to a young hawk as its parent is to an old one; so that general rather than special deception may be the object of this remarkable resemblance, which occurs to a certain extent in many parasitic cuckoos, including the familiar bird at home (*Cuculus canorus*). This also occurs here, and may be heard any spring day at Darjeeling, together with a larger mountaineering relative of the brain-fever bird (*Hierococcyx sparverioides*). India, indeed, rejoices in a number of cuckoos, both of the sort "as doesn't lay 'is own eggs 'isself," and of the more honest section who behave in domestic matters like any ordinary bird. About Calcutta one may occasionally meet, of the former kind, the handsome black and white Crested Cuckoo (*Coccystes jacobinus*) which the natives *will* call a bulbul, and of the latter, the awkward looking Crow-pheasant (*Centropus sinensis*) with its black body and tan wings, which certainly does at first sight recall the two birds whose name it bears rather than the ordinary members of its real family. The Crow-pheasant is prescribed in some places as an enemy to game, which, as his general habits resemble those of a magpie, he probably is; but as he also destroys snakes, it would be better to protect him stringently, since whatever harm he may do to young pheasants or partridges would be in most people's opinion amply offset by warfare on creatures which are their enemies and ours alike.

XVIII.—THE PARROT.

"*Fraught with antics as the Indian bird.*"—*Wordsworth.*

THE Parrot may fairly claim to be *the* Indian bird *par excellence*, for the peacock and fowl had been so long known in Europe, when he arrived to gladden the hearts of Greek bird fanciers, that they had found their way into mythology; and we hardly think of them as foreigners ourselves. But the Parrot, always a captive and renowned for its power of speech, has always remained a type of what is gorgeous, tropical, and strange. This is right enough in a way, for Parrots are very unlike any other birds, European or otherwise, and they are pre-eminently characteristic of warm regions all round the world. But India is not rich in species of Parrots, nor Africa either; the great haunts of these birds are South America and the island continent of Australia and its satellites. And here we see the hardiness of the Parrot constitution; a large parrakeet (*Cyanolyseus patagonus*) haunts the bleak plains of Patagonia; a smaller one (*Cyanorhamphus unicolor*) crawls among the tussock-grass on the remote Antipodes Island, so much in fear of the violent winds which sweep its home that it never takes wing; and it is only high up on the New Zealand Alps that the great sheep-killing Kea (*Nestor notabilis*), which looks as much like a buzzard as a Parrot, makes its horrible meals off living sheep. It would seem therefore that Parrots can live almost anywhere and anyhow, given ground habitable by land-birds at all; and this makes it the more curious that in those most richly varied collections of animal life, the African and Indian faunas, the Parrots make no very great show. We have here no gorgeous lories or macaws, no snowy and crested cockatoos —hardly anything, in fact, but the long-tailed green parrakeets, of which our common Ring-necked species (*Palæornis torquatus*), is far the most abundant, and extends all over India, spreading East to Cochin China. It does not ascend the hills as a rule, and it likes cultivated ground, where it has the opportunity of using holes in buildings, as well as in trees, for nesting purposes, paying for the accommodation afforded by constituting itself an economic pest of the first water by its greedy and wasteful assaults on grain and fruit. It must be admitted, however, as an extenuating circumstance, that "poor Polly's" popularity as a cage-bird outweighs a good deal of damage done, for a good many rupees must be turned over annually by those who deal in Parrots. Hundreds of the birds, both old and young, come into the market annually, and seem to find a ready sale, and certainly this Parrot is the commonest pet bird here, and is very popular in Europe also. In Calcutta, as everyone must have noticed, it is as frequently chained as caged, often, alas, with a chain which would hold an ordinary terrier! Poor Polly indeed! a heavy chain and an iron swing, or a small hemispherical cage, form a sad exchange for the tree tops and the blue sky. Somehow I always pity a caged Parrot now, although Parrots do so well in cages, and their slow crawling movements seem so excellently suited for a captive's narrow bounds.

But a wild Parrot shows one that half the bird's time is passed in its swift graceful flight—a flight, by the way, that is strikingly different from that of most land birds, the downward-pointed wings, with their sharp decisive stroke, at once recalling some plover, sandpiper or other shore-haunting fowl. Like these aquatics, also, Polly carries her feet stowed astern and not tucked up to the breast, though it took me a long time to find this out when I was investigating this point, with a view to discovering the reason for this difference in habit in birds—for some kinds carry their feet forward and others behind in the most inexplicable way. But one day a Parrot, urged perhaps by a desire to examine its defunct relatives, came into the Bird gallery of the museum, and, as it careered to and fro overhead, it gave me an opportunity of seeing how the feet were placed. Ordinarily they seem to be buried in the under-tail-coverts when the bird is on the wing, but this individual was too flurried to put this final touch to its flying attitude. As to the reason, I have not found that out yet; all birds belonging to a given natural family seem to stow their feet in the same way, so that it is probably only a meaningless inherited habit.

Parrots are chiefly winter birds with us in Calcutta, but they must breed not far off, for some of the infants brought into the Provision Bazaar are very young indeed, and hardly fit to stand a long journey. Nasty little things they are, some as naked as the palm of one's hand, and of much the same colour. Few, however, are quite nude, for, as a rule, the green feathers are beginning to sprout before they are taken and brought in. The fledged young bird can be always known from the old one by its dark eyes, a point to be borne in mind by those who are buying Parrots as pets; the old bird's eyes are white—that is to say, their iris is, clearly showing off the waxing and waning pupil which gives the bird such a knowing, wicked look. There is probably some meaning in this expression, for light eyes in birds are often indicative of a bad disposition in their owners; the yellow-eyed Black-crested Yellow Bulbul (*Otocompsa flaviventris*) is much more spiteful than its common dark-eyed relations; and any falconer knows that the yellow-eyed short-winged hawks, such as the goshawk and sparrow-hawk, have much less manageable tempers than the true falcons, which are all dark-eyed.

In spite of her "canister look in the heye," however, Polly makes a nice pet, and is often an excellent talker. The only Indian Parrot I ever actually heard talk was a specimen at a bird show at home, which constantly, marked in a thin piping, but very clear voice "Waiter bring Polly pint of beer, quick, quick, quick!" This was a hen bird, and so I conclude that the sex is not of prime importance in a talking Parrot. As most people know, the male of our common Parrot can be easily distinguished by the pink ring round his neck, which, however, is not found in the newly-fledged bird, but is a sign of maturity. Curiously enough, this pink ring remains in the *lutino* or yellow variety, which is not uncommon, and sells for a high price. It certainly is a most lovely bird, being of a most even and delicate yellow, and retaining the bright red bill of the ordinary green bird. Among the wild green birds brought into Tiretta Bazaar—presumably for sale to the guileless sailor—one often sees specimens more or less heavily splashed with yellow, and probably by pairing these the pure yellow form could be bred at will in a few generations. In the only observed case known to me of the actual production of this variety, however, I am told that the parents are just two ordinary green Parrots; they breed every year in the same tree and all their brood are always yellow, and a lively competition exists among the local natives for the position of these valuable youngsters.

It is a very curious fact that, popular as the Parrot has always been as a pet, the native fanciers have never attempted to breed this "sport' in confinement; whereas in the case of the little Australian Grass Parrakeet or "Budgerigar" (*Melopsittacus undulatus*) which has only been known as a cage-bird in Europe for about half a century, a yellow variety has already been fixed, and is now offered for sale at a price doubtless highly gratifying to its producers. The Budgerigar is a familiar cage-bird here and has even escaped and bred, but it has not yet, at all events, established itself as one of our wild birds.

Our own native bird is certainly not very conspicuous here at most times, and I was astonished to find him so abundant in Bombay, where he is as numerous as the mynah in Calcutta. The Parrot, however, will make his presence felt wherever he is. and his familiar squeal overhead is one of the pleasantest sounds of a cold-weather morning. It is a curious fact that Parrots do not in their wild state indulge their imitative faculties at all. unlike the clever starling tribe; and so thousands of generations of them live and die in their native jungles without ever fully exercising ears and tongue fully as acute, in many cases, as our own. I say tongue conventionally, of course, for in Parrots, as in other birds, the tongue has nothing to do with the production of the sounds uttered, human or otherwise; the bird's vocal organ being the *syrinx*, which is situated at the base of the windpipe, where that organ forks before entering the lungs.

I have not seen any other kind of Parrot wild about here, but the large "Rock Parrot" (*Palæornis nepalensis*) is said to occur in that condition, and is at all events such a very common captive as to require notice. In the difference between different sexes and ages, and in its general colour and form it resembles the ordinary Parrot, but it is not only larger, but of a much duller green, and always possesses a splash of red on the wing. Its plumage never seems to incline to yellow like the smaller Parrot's, although we have in the museum a skin of the very nearly allied Andaman large Parrot ((*Palæornis magnirostris*) which is nearly a pure "lutino." This Andaman variety chiefly differs in having a very much bigger bill, according to a very general rule in island colonists among birds; but why an insular habitat should result in a big nose is a problem which science has yet to solve.

XIX.—THE OWL.

"*The Owl and Owlet........talking, scolding, at each other.*"—*Longfellow.*

THE ordinary notes of our common little spotted Owlet (*Athene brama*) do certainly suggest family jars, the spasmodic cackles in which it indulges before beginning its nightly avocations sounding as if promoted by very bad feeling. But, as a matter of fact, the house Owlet is a harmless and not unsociable little being; I have seen one "playing gooseberry" to a pair of lovers of its own species with the utmost nonchalance, and, up-country, where it comes out in broad daylight, the other birds generally do not seem to mind its presence, though I once saw one being hustled by the "sat-bhai." In Calcutta, however, the Owls do not appear till the shades of night have pretty well fallen, doubtless on account of the crows, who, numbering among their very few foes the large horned Owls, persecute all the tribe on principle; for how are they to know that the small Owls won't grow up into big ones? We are far too apt to fall into the mistake that birds are born with an intimate knowledge of ornithology; that is a subject they have to study just as much as ourselves. No doubt the *small* birds suffer from the little Owl at times, but generally insects, mice, and house-lizards must make up his bill of fare, as being most easily obtainable. He is not a bird of powerful flight, and does not spend much time on the wing, his up-and-down method of travelling not being suited for hunting; so he prefers to sit on a telegraph-wire, or any other convenient perch, and await eventualities.

He is very much of a domestic Owl, and I am told, is sometimes so tame in verandahs where he is unmolested that he will let himself be touched; for under man's hospitable roof he finds a dormitory for the day-time, and a convenient nesting place. The few eggs his mate lays are white, like those of all Owls, and the fluffy owlets, when fledged, are drab-and-white with yellow eyes just like their parents, for as a general rule Owls do not go in for invidious distinctions between different sexes and ages in the matter of dress. In Burma and Western India, the little Owls are smaller and darker than hereabout; and in the north-west, about Peshawar, begins the range of another species, the Bactrian Owlet (*Athene bactriana*) chiefly differing from the Indian bird in being streaked instead of barred below. This bird is almost identical with the celebrated Owl of Minerva (*Athene noctua*), which must have been as common in Athens as *Athene brama* is here, since "to take owls to Athens" was the classical equivalent for taking coals to Newcastle. Minerva's Owl was, of course, the bird of wisdom, and by their selection the Greeks showed their own discernment, for Owls are anything but the futile creatures which popular tradition makes them to be both here and at home. An Owl combines valour with discretion; his nest is more dangerous to rob than a hawk's, while as to his habits by day he may well say with Diomed "thou dost miscall retire; I do not fly, but advantageous care withdrew me from the odds of multitude,'' for he can see well enough in the daytime, but is perfectly conscious of his unpopularity with other birds. Moreover, Owls are prudent and far-seeing, even to laying up a store of food against time of dearth; not that our local owlet has any need to do this, as he never goes into cold climates. In America, however, the small horned-owl (*Scops asio*) has been found gloating over a store of fresh fish, which he had taken advantage of an artificial opening in the ice to procure from a pond a mile off! That Owls should fish seems unnatural, somehow, and yet we have more than one fishing species in India, and the ordinary "mousing owl" of barn and steeple has been known to turn piscator in England.

The said Barn-owl (*Strix flammea*) is also found in Calcutta, but is not nearly so conspicuous as the little spotted bird, and is comparatively seldom seen, owing, no doubt, to his more nocturnal habits. Now and then one may see the big broad-winged bird flapping steadily and silently over the compound, or plunging into a bush to raid the roosting sparrows, for this Owl is one of the enemies of those pestilential finches, although his more ordinary diet consists of "rats and mice and such small deer." For the capture of these he is eminently adapted; his dark eyes look out from a most perfectly-formed "facial disk," that radiating arrangement of feathers so beautifully contrived to concentrate the light—though the immediate effect of the Barn-owl's heart-shaped countenance on most people is to make them compare him to a monkey; his wings are longer than in other Owls, to sustain him in his search over open ground for his victims, as he is not migratory; and his legs are also long, presumably for convenience in a sudden grapple, since he is not a quick or elegant pedestrian, his long talons being to grip with, not to walk on. There is one point about the Barn-owl's structure, however, that badly needs explanation, and that is the small-tooth-comb which he carries on the inner side of his middle claw. It is true that all birds use this particular claw for scratching their heads with, and that some other species besides this Owl have a similar arrangement; but nature has distributed the favour with a niggard and partial hand, and in a manner that at present defies conjecture.

But his structural peculiarities are not the only points about the Barn-owl; he teems with interest. For one thing, he is one of the most cosmopolitan of birds, being found practically everywhere except in the high north and in New Zealand; he varies in colour and size to an extent which has given naturalists a great deal of trouble, for several beautiful species could be made out of him if his progeny would stick to one type. But this they will not do; once in Calcutta I had two fine young birds of the same age, and presumably the same brood, of which one had a white face and breast, while the other's breast was buff, and its face smoky grey. Both were spotted with black below, which is usual with the Barn-owl here, whereas in England the bird's waistcoat is plain. The English Barn-owl also tends to sport a white tail, the Indian bird's being buff with dark bars. But then the same bird in Jamaica comes out with the points of the English form, thus upsetting a beautiful rule that might otherwise be framed to the effect that "insular tropical forms of this owl are very dark." The Andaman Barn-owl certainly bears out the rule to the letter, but as it is also conspicuous by having very much shorter wings than the continental birds, while the bill and feet are just as big if not bigger, it may really be a distinct species altogether. This raises the interesting question as to whether the dark insular-tropical Owls of this kind are a primitive race like the small dark human races which have a way of cropping up in out-of-the-way places, or whether the Barn-owl when it gets on a tropical island proceeds with singular uniformity to degenerate in complexion and power of wing. One might argue a point like this till doomsday, and so as the Barn-owl is an eminently useful bird, it is fortunate that he has been introduced into New Zealand, which is sufficiently insular, if not tropical; there he can evolve for such of our great-grandsons as take an interest in natural history.

Unfortunately, and this another point of interest about the Barn-owl, he is not popular. Owls, generally speaking, are considered uncanny as well as stupid; and the Barn-owl, both in Europe and in India, is the worst reputed of the lot. From Spenser, who called him "the rueful shrick, still waiting on the bere," to the modern Spaniard, who thinks he is of the devil's poultry and drinks the oil out of church lamps, his reputation has been hopelessly bad in the west. And out here the native calls him the "bad bird" or "death-bird," and dreads his weird screech accordingly; but he does not kill him wantonly or for the purpose of mounting him as a hand-screen. The use of the owl to the native consists in his various magical properties, chief of which is the fact that if you serve him up instead of chicken in a curry the hapless partaker thereof will become as stupid as an owl, a consummation devoutly to be wished in the case of an enemy !

XX.—THE VULTURE.

Never stoops the soaring vulture

. . . .

But another vulture, watching
From his high aerial lookout,
Sees the downward plunge, and follows·
And a third pursues the second,
Coming from the invisible ether,
First a speck, and then a vulture,
Till the air is dark with pinions.—Longfellow.

THE length of the above quotation will, I am sure, be excused for the sake of its beauty and accuracy; for it is now well established that Vultures find their food not by scent, as some authors use to maintain, but by sight only. Nor is it necessarily the case that a Vulture should discover it at all; often the ubiquitous crow is the first comer, only to be driven off by the kite, who in turn yields place to his betters. The commonest Vulture hereabout is certainly the Bengal or white-backed species (*Pseudogyps bengalensis*), which may be seen almost any day soaring high in air, his wings flat and motionless as boards, in hope of the full meal that he gets, perhaps, once a week. For when a carcase is found, and the Vultures are assembled to enjoy it, they quarrel a good deal over the repast, and many have to stand back before their despot, the King Vulture (*Otogyps calvus*), who keeps the plebians off till he is satisfied; though even he fears the great Adjutant Stork (*Leptoptilus dubius*), once so common in Calcutta, but now, alas! only a memory. The Bengal Vulture is a dull dirty-looking bird of a dingy black, relieved only by some white on the back and under the wing, and this only noticeable in flight. The regal bird, which is not nearly so numerous, is of a richer blackness, and has a bright red head, with a pendent flap on each side, as the insignia of his rank. The young of both are of a dirty brown, and in this resemble our third local species, the Long-billed Vulture (*Gyps tenuirostris*), which is, however, easily distinguishable by its very long and lean head and neck; it is quite a grey-hound among Vultures. The best place to study vultures and their want of manners is at Dhappa, to which richly-flavoured locality I once made an expedition for that purpose. Here the Bengal Vultures fare somewhat meagrely on the boiled garbage thrown out from the vats after the town carcases of horse and bullock have been boiled down for grease; and as they are nearly as tame as turkeys they can be easily watched. The Long-billed birds are few and more shy; they keep aloof, disdaining, as I was told, boiled beef in the hope of a more dainty meal of dead dogs and rats. To these viands the King Vulture appears also more addicted, but I saw none at Dhappa and was told they were rare there and much more wary than the rest. In fact, the first occasion on which I identified his vulturine highness in Calcutta was when two of the species pitched on the maidan, apparently to settle some difference of opinion. Since then I have seen one or two others there.

In Vultures we have in the East not only the rajah and the common ruck of his subjects of various species, but the humble sweeper, in the form of the well-known White Scavenger Vulture (*Neophron ginginianus*). This bird, however, eschewed the neighbourhood of Calcutta, for although appallingly accommodating of stomach, he has some delicacy of constitution about him, and avoids a moist climate.

It is a curious thing that the same hierarchy of Vultures obtains in America, although the birds there belong to a distinct family of their own; the old-world vultures being very near of kin to the eagles. In South America we get a handsome and powerful King Vulture (*Cathartes papa*), but creamy-fawn is here the royal colour; and he has for subjects the mean Turkey-Buzzards (*Oenops aura*), in their rusty black, and the Gallinazos or Black Vultures (*Cathariste atratus*), which look uncommonly like our scavenger, only dipped in ink, the colours of sovereign and sweeper being practically reversed. It is a curious fact that the Old and New World Vultures, like the monkeys of the two worlds, can most readily be separated by the form of the nostrils; the difference in the case of the birds being that in the Eastern Vultures there is a partition between the nostrils as in most animals, whereas in the Western family this is absent, and you can look right through the beak from one side to the other. The American Vultures also have weaker feet and do not build nests; and they have no voice-muscles, so that they can only hiss. Their Eastern relatives, though not taloned like eagles, are more powerful in the extremities, and even carry nesting material therewith, for they build large unwieldy nests on trees or rocks; and they are sufficiently well endowed with a vocal apparatus to vent their affections in horrid bellowings at the breeding season. Our Vultures here build large rough nests in trees, of fresh boughs torn off by main strength, and the plebeians are sociable, nesting in colonies; royalty, of course, can tolerate no neighbouring rivals. As a rule, they only lay one egg; a large fertility is not necessary to keep up the numbers of birds which run so few risks as Vultures do and possess such iron constitutions. They have even been known to take and survive doses of poison which would inevitably have proved fatal to anything else.

A pleasing subject for speculation is the baldness of these disreputable fowl. Of course the most obvious explanation is that feathers on a head which is continually being poked inside carcases would soon be the reverse of ornamental, if not unhealthy; but as Darwin, with his usual philosophic caution, remarks, the head of the cleanly turkey is just as naked. So are those of the Ibis and the Cassowary, and the Sarus Crane, and scattered here and there throughout the bird class we come upon heads grievously in need of a hair restorer. It will, however, be noticed, that such usually belong to *big* birds; and that where degrees of baldness exist in any given family, the biggest will also generally be the barest on the top. The Ostrich indeed, the largest of all birds, is also the nakedest; his head and neck only have scanty hairs, and his thighs are completely nude. To apply this to the Vulture; the low-caste and under-sized Scavenger has a bald face, the ordinary Vultures a sparsely downy head and neck, the Longbilled a longer and nakeder neck, and the King luxuriates in complete bald-headedness accentuated by side-flaps, and a naked red patch inside each thigh. A very similar gradation may also be traced with the American kinds. So, too, with the cranes. The little Demoiselle (*Anthropoides virgo*) has her pretty head well covered; the Coolung (*Grus communis*) is much bigger and is bare on the top; the white Crane (*Grus leucogeranus*), bigger still, is bare trom beak to eyes all round; and the great Sarus is naked all over his head and some way down his neck. Thus we arrive at the fact that baldness and prosperity in birds somehow go together; when a species gets up in the world it can afford to take off some of its feathers where they will not be missed, and go about more or less décolleté. A simpler explanation would be that when a bird gets over a certain size it can't grow enough feathers to cover itself properly; but after all this involves the other, for it must be prosperous to be big at all. Vultures may certainly claim to be well-to-do, though they don't look it. Their simple tastes are more easily gratified than the expensive ones of the eagles, who, however, will condescend to bully the best of them occasionally in order to take of their high yet humble repast; and nobody owes them a grudge, for they do no one any harm to speak of. Yet there are curious limits to their spread which are hard to understand. It is strange that there should be none in Ceylon, for instance, and that none inhabit Australia; for though not migratory, they are great travellers on occasion—the Arabs of North Africa said that during the

Crimean War the Vultures emigrated to Europe with an eye to unlimited dead horse. They can bear both heat and cold, and the only hindrance they would be likely to meet, one would think, would be heavy jungle in which they could not see their food. The New World birds are more enterprising, for the Turkey Buzzard extends from end to end, almost, of the American Continent and is a well known bird everywhere. It is true that one of the Old World birds, the huge Cinereous Vulture (*Vultur monachus*) also spreads from Spain to China, but it is not a common species anywhere, so that there must be some check on its increase that does not exist in the case of the much weaker and smaller Turkey-Buzzard, which is a very insignificant bird compared to it. But nothing demonstrates better than the study of the lives of birds that the battle is not always to the strong. The Turkey Buzzard in Jamaica has itself been recently experiencing a serious and quite unexpected check by reason of the introduction of one of our best known Indian animals, the mongoose. This beast plays havoc with the eggs of the poor Vulture, which has not, so far, developed sufficient sense to move his domestic belongings to a safer situation than the bare ground and has become much less numerous in consequence. It is evident therefore that "John Crow," as the Turkey Buzzard is called, has not intelligence equal to his constitution, and that he has prospered so far more by luck than judgment.

XXI.—THE KITE.

"*When the kite builds look to lesser linen.*"—*Shakespeare.*

The Kite is a melancholy example of unutilized talents. He could, if he chose to exert himself, be monarch of all he surveyed in Calcutta, but he lets the crow get there before him every time. You never see a crow miss the opportunity of annoying a Kite, but what does the Kite do in retaliation? He essays a few robberies with violence, it is true; but only once, and that after several years' residence here, have I seen him successful. Usually the pursued crow "puts in," as a falconer would say, to a house or tree in time to save his bacon or whatever else he has appropriated. Indeed, I have seen him settle down to peck at his booty, held firmly under his foot, before the baffled Kite had wheeled away. That the kite can be formidable if he likes anyone may find out who cares to stroll out on a verandah with an unconcerned expression and anything edible—or that a kite's experience of human habits leads him to think may be so. The experimenter will find that an unseen bird will sweep down from behind and whip the object of experiment out of his hand before he can say whatever he is in the habit of saying on occasions of unpleasant surprise. "There's many a slip 'twixt the cup and the lip" was once admirably exemplified to me by a Kite. I was imprudently drinking tea in the open when I felt a flap on my nose, and the cup was rudely dashed to the ground—but I never saw the kite; nor is this the only occasion on which a kite burglariously attacked me—in fact, I kept always ready for them latterly. Their dexterity is something marvellous; never have I been scratched by their talons, though I have had bread snatched out of my very hand. It is this wonderful management of wing and foot that makes the kite, in spite of his shabby brown plumage and general appearance as of a small eagle run to seed, such a beautiful and interesting bird to watch at his task of scavenging. Whatever his mark is, he always takes it with his feet, and holding it therein, he will, if the object be small enough, and his companions do not interfere, dine on it in mid-air. So rooted is this habit that when he is making a light supper on the delicious and succulent white-ant as it swarms, he ceremoniously seizes even this minute prey in one foot instead of snapping it up with his bill. The only time he breaks his rule of "feet before bill" is when he is carrying sticks for his nest, at which time he may often be seen with his load in his beak. This seems a peculiarly senseless habit, but it is quite possible that the Kite's idea is to have his feet free for fighting, for he relies on his talons rather than his bill in this also. Everyone has seen how, of two bickering Kites, the lower bird will turn on his back to receive the swoop of the upper, till with locked talons they go slowly spinning towards the ground; generally having sense enough to let go before they reach it, however. On the ground the Kite is not at home; he walks in a stiff-legged fashion, and gets under way with some difficulty, like most long-winged birds; and as he wants a lot of room for his evolutions, he has little use for trees, except to perch on the top of them. He seems, indeed, when nesting, to favour buildings much more than the crow, no doubt for this reason.

I have not observed in the kite's matrimonial arrangement that refined delicacy which has been alluded to in the case of the crow. Endearments and presents seem to be at a discount, and the banns of marriage are published abroad by an aggravation of the ordinary virulent squealing which is to my mind the Kite's worst fault as a town bird. Ornamental, except in flight, he certainly is not, though he seems to have an idea that he is suited for mural decoration, judging from the way in which he spread-eagles himself against any warm wall. The young Kite is indeed handsomely spotted with buff after he has grown out of his white nestling-down—for young Kites are not indecently nude like young crows—but when this ultimately gives place to the sombre snuff-colour of the adult bird, there is little for the æsthetic eye to take hold of. But the Kite may fairly claim to be both useful and harmless. Garbage of any sort, from a dead rat to a footful of boiled rice, he will appropriate and make away with, if not robbed of it by the crows; and he cannot very well do much harm, as anything with any sense knows how to get out of his way. Moreover, he is an arrant coward as a rule, though bolder in defence of his nest than the crow, whose parental affection is apt to be overborne by a prudent distrust of his powers of flight; a Kite's nest is not to be approached without caution if one does not want to be clawed over the scalp.

The Kite's most unpleasant habit is that of eating his prey alive—a trait which marks him as a bird accustomed to tackle what can't hit him back; since the "nobler" hawks have, in self-defence, to kill their more powerful quarry, as quickly as possible. Altogether he is not a nice bird, and one can quite understand how when tame falcons and wild Kites were well known to our ancestors, the name of the latter bird became a common term of abuse. For the Kite was once as common in England as in India: a Bohemian visitor noticed in the fifteenth century that he had never seen so many Kites anywhere as round London Bridge—an observation that throws a lurid light on the City sanitation. The common European Kite, however, is not exactly the same bird as his relative here. *Milvus govinda*, our urban sanitator, is smaller than *Milvus ictinus* of Europe, which is much redder in colour, especially on the tail, and whiter on the head—in fact a finer bird altogether.

This bird, despised as he was generally, was royal game in falconry; for, coward as the Kite is, to capture him taxes the powers of a falcon to the utmost, and one that could perform the feat was deemed fit for "a prince's pleasant sport." The Kite when pursued by the falcon "takes the sky," and both birds rise to a great height, the quarry endeavouring, as long as he may, to shift from the fatal grip of his more powerful enemy. Indeed, in one case in which King James I. was induced personally to witness the flight at a Kite of a couple of falcons which had been procured for him, both pursuers and pursued went out of sight altogether and permanently, an extreme form of the diversion which could hardly have been pleasing to the parsimonious prince, for the birds had cost a thousand pounds to procure, being so remarkably good that they had taken nine Kites running without a miss.

With the advance of sanitation and the decay of falconry the English Kite began to be looked on solely as a nuisance. Cuffs and collars were not safe when he was furnishing his nest, as Shakespeare knew, and many young chickens fell victims to his insidious attacks. At the same time, there has been no reason to shoot and trap him so mercilessly as has been done, making the Kite one of the rarest of British birds. But as the Indian Kite has the whole of India to range over, and goes even as far as Australia, no amount of sanitation, poultry-breeding, or game-preserving, is likely to bring him anywhere near extermination. Talking of the Kite's residence, it is curious that Jerdon alludes to a story that they leave Calcutta almost entirely during the rains, which, Dr. Blanford says, is perfectly correct. How such an idea could have arisen I do not know. I have always noticed Kites in the rains, and have never heard that they ever were in the habit of leaving Calcutta then. This Kite is not usually migratory, unlike the big Kite of the hills (*Milvus melanotis*) which may be distinguished by its white instead of yellow feet, white patch under the wing, and larger size, the male hill-kite being as big as or bigger than the female of our low-country bird. Females in Kites, it should be observed, are larger than males, following the usual but inexplicable rule of birds of prey.

Milvus melanotis, as one sees him at Darjeeling, is certainly a finer bird altogether than our Calcutta cockney, but both are thrown into the shade by another common Calcutta resident, the Brahminy Kite (*Haliastur indus*). It is rather an insult to class this bird with the kites, for he is, at all events, of a much better *jat*, as his name implies, though Tommy, having converted the same name into "Bromley-kite," applies it to the common pariah bird. In his first plumage, indeed, the Brahminy Kite is very like the adult pariah, but may be easily distinguished by his rounded tail—the other's being forked in the old and square in the young—and by "a certain indefinable style." When he becomes adult, however, there is no possible confusion, the Brahminy's brilliant chestnut, set off by black quills and a white head, being quite unique among Indian birds of prey. To see the Brahminy one has usually to go down the Hooghly, for he is not much of a town bird, though I used to see one not unfrequently at the Museum tank. He is said to be a bolder bird than the common Kite, and to rob this bird of its prey. Other birds fear him little as a rule, however; I have seen one perched on a bush with several paddy-birds, and a kingfisher has been known to "wipe the eye" of a Brahminy in the matter of a fish the latter was stooping to seize. In this case, however, the small bird paid dearly for his impudence, for the indignant bird of prey vindictively hunted him down and devoured him alive!

The Brahminy reminds one rather of the American Bird o'Freedom, and indeed he is rather a dwarf sea-eagle than a Kite. Curiously enough there are no Kites, properly so called, in America, for the birds so styled by American ornithologists do not seem particularly like what we associate with the name in the Old World. One can understand that the carrion-hawks would stand in their way in South America, but it is difficult to understand why they have not spread into the fine field for emigration offered by the top half of the great Western continent.

Spotted Dove.

Turtur suratensis.

XXII.—THE DOVE.

"*The love of the turtle.*"—*Byron.*

MR. PHIL ROBINSON, in his delightfully humorous book "Noah's Ark," arrives at the conclusion that the lion takes rank as king of the beasts because he roars loudest; and similarly the Dove seems to have gained credit as the truest and most typical lover among the birds, because he makes the most fuss about his affections. At any rate the fancy of our spotted Turtle-dove (*Turtur suratensis*) seems to turn to thoughts of love the whole year round. Any day you may see him bowing profoundly to the object of his adoration and inflating his speckled neck as he gives forth his rather harsh and unmelodious coo. For, as a cooer, he does not compare at all favourably with another Dove very familiar in Calcutta, the domestic fawn-coloured or white Dove, which is so well-known as a cage-bird, although its real origin and home seem to be still doubtful. The spotted Dove, however, has few rivals among the Turtle-doves in the matter of plumage, being most elegantly spotted with pinkish fawn on a drab ground, and boasting a black tippet spotted with white as a neck ornament. As is usual with Doves, the male and female are equally pretty, but the young birds have no tippet-marking at first, and only a dingy indication of the pretty speckling on the back, which will appear later. The eggs whence the twin offspring are disclosed are white, as in all Doves, and deposited on a flimsy collection of twigs, placed, doubtless, in some secure retreat; for, in spite of the numbers of doves to be seen about suitable compounds, their nests are not by any means common objects, and, considering the proverbial helplessness of "two strengthless doves," it is really very creditable to the pretty pairs that they bring off so many young. Love, indeed, supplies much to these weak creatures, giving them courage not only to fight each other with their feeble bills and unarmed wings, but even to attack the blackguard crow, even if not, as Shakespeare says, to "peck the estridge." They are the best of parents, too; if the wild cock dove is like his tame relative, he is a most admirable husband and father, taking his fair share of the sitting, *i.e.*, most of the day time, and feeding his young just as assiduously as their mother does; first with the "pigeon's milk" secreted in the crop, and afterwards with softened grain and other vegetable food.

The vegetarian habits of the Doves, and their want of special weapons for fighting and of means of defence, have no doubt given them their reputation for gentleness, which is really hardly deserved, in respect of their relations to each other. Harmless to other birds not of their own species or family they undoubtedly are; but among themselves, and with other members of the tribe, the Doves generally display a spirit of nagging which leads one to suspect that the author, who spoke of the "mild, humble, patient, peaceful dove" had never made the acquaintance of the bird outside a pigeon-pie. The terms "pigeon" and "dove" seem to have originally been, to a certain extent, interchangeable; but now the latter term has been confined in use almost exclusively to the smaller members of the family, such as our present subject. Mild, then, the Dove certainly is not, but a most inveterate pugilist in a feeble way; and he can hardly be called patient, in consideration of the way in which a new-caught bird will knock itself about in captivity; although the species can be so far reconciled to that condition as to propagate itself therein, as happened some years ago in the London Zoological Gardens. As to humility, that can hardly be assigned as a conspicuous quality of birds so given to bloating and bowing and scraping as are the Doves. They are all, taken as a family, given to this form of ostentation; but the turtle group have also a very pretty form of showing off which is very characteristic of them. This consists in the bird towering up in the air for a short distance, and then sailing downward with outspread tail, so as to show off the light and dark marking of the under surface thereof to the fair spectator below.

I have seen this done by several wild species, and also by a tame bird, to which I used occasionally to allow a little liberty; and this shows the persistence of the instinct, for the quarters in which such tame Doves are usually kept are not so spacious as to afford facilities for the performance. But nothing is more striking than the fidelity with which individuals of a species, or various naturally allied species, will reproduce the same attitudes in courtship, showing the essentially artless and instinctive nature of the performance. Thus, all the Turtle-doves, when bowing, keep their tail closed, not spreading it as the pigeon does, though they have just as much, if not more, reason for doing so, as the closure prevents the light side feathers from being seen.

The Turtle-doves, however, may well be tenacious of their customs, for they are a prosperous clan, albeit confined to the Old World, and mostly to the warmer parts thereof; but their conjugal and parental devotion enables them to increase rapidly in spite of individual feebleness and small broods, and wherever they occur they are common birds as a rule. Only a few migrate, but our only English species, the traditional and original Turtle-dove (*Turtur communis*), is a thriving migrant which is continually extending its range northward. The Spotted Dove s a short-winged bird compared with this and is one of our resident and most characteristic birds in India; in Burma its place is taken by a very near ally, the Malay Spotted Dove (*Turtur tigrinus*), which is less distinctly spotted, while further east, in China, we get another species (*Turtur chinensis*) which is not spotted at all, although it bears a black-and-white tippet like the other two.

Another Dove that may sometimes, but not often, be met with in Calcutta is the Ring-dove (*Turtur risorius*), a bird very like the tame Dove, but drab instead of fawn in colour. Indeed, as the tame bird appears to be sometimes coloured just like the wild one, one might put it down as the descendant of the latter, were it not that the coo of the two birds is different. It may be urged in this connection that there is a difference in the song of the white tame and the grey wild Java sparrows; but in these ring-necked Turtle-doves the notes of the various wild species are so distinct that the coo becomes a character of importance. The wild Ring-dove never seems to utter the peculiar sniggering laugh of the tame one, which is quite unlike any note made by any other turtle-dove I know, and I have studied several in life. Whether or not it gave origin to the world-familiar domestic pet, the Ring-dove of India has a wide range on its own account, and may soothe with its cooing the ears of many men of many races from the unspeakable Turk in Europe to the heathen Chinese in the uttermost East.

XXIII.—THE GULL.

"*Sauntering hither on listless wings.*"—*Bret Harte.*

For some reason or other, the warmer seas are not rich in species of Gulls, and so these graceful birds are not so numerous with us as one used to European sea-ports would expect to find them. Indeed, all round the wide extent of the coasts of the Indian Empire not nearly so many Gulls are found as have been recorded from the British Islands; and in our part of India only one species can be called really common. This is the Brown-headed Gull (*Larus brunneicephalus*), a familiar enough object to any one who keeps his eyes open when in sight of the Hooghly during a large part of the year. After the hot weather has well set in, however, it leaves us for the high regions of Central Asia, where it breeds, though no one has as yet been lucky enough to take the eggs, which are therefore as yet undescribed. It is not likely, however, that they will be very different from the usual brown and spotted type found in the family.

It is only just before it leaves us that the Gull dons its brown hood, and its general plumage, of white below and French-grey above, is so much of a family livery that it would not be very distinctive if there were several species to be confounded together here. But this is not the case, for the only other Gull one is at all likely to see in Calcutta is a familiar home bird, the Laughing Gull (*Larus ridibundus*), so abundant and tame in Scotland, and reputed to be the producer of many of the "Plover's eggs" of commerce. This bird is, however, slightly smaller than the commoner Indian one, has dark instead of light eyes, and—a much more noticeable distinction—the longest flight-feathers, forming the tip of the wing, mostly white, while in the bigger bird these are chiefly black. By this the young birds also may be distinguished; in both species they are much like each other, having the upper plumage more brown than grey, and a broad black band at the end of the tail. Moreover, their legs and bills are only coloured orange, instead of the rich deep red which adorns these parts in the old birds. As in all Gulls, there is no difference in plumage between male and female. But, like the pigeons, in which a similar equality usually exists, Gulls are very demonstrative in their courtships, as may be seen in the captive birds at the Alipore Zoo. The attitude which the enamoured Gull apparently considers most attractive is an arched neck and wings opened in front, while kept close at the tips, and no doubt it does as well as any other, for the whole family carry all their delicate beauty of colour fully exposed, not having, like so many birds, hidden charms to display. For they are better off than the dwellers on land as regards enemies; their easy, lazy looking flight is yet well calculated to puzzle a hawk, and their habit of flocking at their breeding places makes for protection when their helpless offspring need it. Helpless comparatively, that is to say, for the young Gull, although it does not run about and find its own food like a young duck, is yet open-eyed and downy, and able to get about and look after itself to some extent; thus being an interesting link between the active chick and the blind naked helpless nestlings of so many birds. The brown-mottled plumage, which is the first feathering of the young Gull, is also probably a protection, while it gains strength of wing and experience, for, as one may see at home, where so many Gulls are bred, it makes the young bird much harder to see when on the shore than is the old one in its grey and white dress.

Another advantage Gulls have in the struggle for existence is their readiness of resource; their ease and grace of flight is patent to every observer, and though they are not very swift on the wing, they can easily follow and circle round a steamer. On the land they run about actively, without the usual waddle of a water-fowl, but with a pretty mincing gait peculiarly their own; and on the water they sit lightly and gracefully, though they do not swim very fast and cannot usually dive at all. In case of need, they perch readily enough, though their feet are not suited for taking a grip of anything, and they have to rely upon balance.

Above all, they are very easily accommodated with food; fish they like when they can get it, but they are not very clever fishers, and their best opportunity is when the hapless fry are hard beset by the bigger members of the class below, and are not in a condition to look after themselves; and so they fall back on insect and vegetable food and garbage of various sorts, including especially what is thrown overboard from ships and fishing-boats. It may be that their scarcity in warm seas is due to the comparative rarity of ships and fishing stations therein; but, it is also very possible that heat does not suit most Gulls' constitutions. At any rate, two non-Indian species, the common Gull (*Larus canus*) and the Great Black-backed Gull (*Larus marinus*), did not thrive in captivity at the Alipore Zoo, where the Brown-headed Gull and its smaller relative have done very well.

Whether from their greater ability to provide for themselves piscatorially, or from a heat-enduring nature, the Gulls' graceful relatives, the Terns, are quite at home in the Tropics. They certainly prefer warm regions, as they leave Northern Europe in winter, and many breed even in our seas around India. They may be known from Gulls by their usually smaller size, forked tails—whence their alternative name of sea-swallows—and small feet, and their bills are not hooked like those of Gulls. They are constantly on the wing, plunging down with a headlong dash on their prey of small fish and shrimps, or even hunting over the dry land for insects. Most of them are so much alike in colour, being of a delicate grey set off by a black cap, that they are hard to distinguish at a distance; but one species or another may often be seen about Calcutta. I have even noticed them hawking over the museum tank, right in the town. Occasionally in winter they find their way into the Provision Bazaar, where not being ducks or "E-shnipe," they go down as "Peeluver bird" along with other miscellaneous wild fowl. Some of these really are worth eating, but it is hard when the pretty Terns are translated from their proper sphere of landscape ornamentation to ingloriously disfigure a sorry scrap of toast.

XXIV.—THE PADDY-BIRD.

"*The eel's foe the heroun.*"—*Chaucer.*

It is not many cities of this size that can claim a heron of any sort as a resident; but the Pond Heron or Paddy-bird (*Ardeola grayi*) lives and moves and has his being with us always, and is very fairly numerous. Conspicuous he is too, when he spreads his white wings for flight; until then you will probably not notice him at all in most cases. For his drab upper plumage is most admirably protective, and he would well merit the title of the "surprise bird," if the American globe-trotter had not already bestowed that on the Roller or blue-jay. When the breeding season comes on in the rains, however, the Paddy-bird feels that he must be smart at all risks, and goes in for a dun ruff and maroon cloak, an alteration in his appearance that "gives him away" at once. I say "him," but as a matter of fact "her" would be just as correct, for the Paddy-birds, like most of the heron family, show no difference between the sexes, even when they put on a wedding-dress. Young Paddy-birds are drab-and-white like the old ones in winter, though they may be distinguished by the white of the wings being slightly sullied in places. When they are squabs in the nest, their scanty down allows their skin to be seen, and this, curiously enough, is of a light and cheerful green like their legs, and contrasts strikingly with their flesh-coloured beaks. They always have green legs, but the beak, as they grow up, changes to blue and yellow with a black tip. Their eyes too are always yellow like those of most herons, this giving the family a vicious appearance, which their disposition does not belie; for, though sociable at breeding and roosting-time, they are decidedly quarrelsome, ill-conditioned birds in their general character. What every heron wants is to be let alone, and if he feels his liberties and rights are being encroached upon, he does his best to give the intruder "one in the eye" with a despatch and accuracy which are the natural outcome of much fishing experience. The heron tribe are, indeed, specialists in the art of taking aim and biding their time; they do not generally walk about after their prey but wait for it to come to them, and reach for it when it is obliging enough to do so. Their general habits and attitudes are very stereotyped, and any one who has watched the little Paddy-bird will have a very good idea of most of his relatives. They all keep their necks curved back on their shoulders when they are flying, unlike most other long-necked birds; and they mostly fly with the same easy regular stroke of the wings, which, in the case of the bigger species is much quicker than it looks. Twice I have timed the wing-strokes of the big grey heron (*Ardea cinerea*) at home, and both times found them to be two to every second.

They build, too, the same style of nest, a miserable platform of sticks or other convenient material, generally in a tree, like the Paddy-bird, and the eggs are usually light blue like hers. It is their difference from other birds that makes herons so striking and interesting; their usually silent undemonstrative ways, stiff, persistent attitudes, and the strange contrast of their bustle and clamour where they congregate, make them attract every one's attention wherever they are found. Also, though far less graceful in form than many other water-birds, they have the fatal gift of beauty in the form of filmy feathers they bear on their backs as wedding garments; which, in the trade, have somehow got the absurd name of "ospreys." For these the poor birds are ruthlessly shot down, though this has not been done so much in India as in America, where the valuable white-plumed species have been terribly persecuted—and most cruelly, as they carry these plumes all the while they are rearing young. It is fortunate for the Paddy-bird that he does not bear plumage of the first quality, but still he gets indented on to a certain extent. But under the Act that has now been made about bird protection, he will receive all the immunity he needs, for herons are easy birds to legislate about, owing to their distinctness, which makes them always distinguishable, and their unanimity in the matter of places and season for breeding. It is just possible, indeed, that protection may be overdone in case of these fish-eating birds, though not very likely, as they are themselves esteemed as food by some natives. It seems, however, that the Buff-backed Egret (*Bubulcus coromandus*), which forms so picturesque an object in the landscape as he stalks by the dark buffaloes, is tabooed by certain fastidious Mussulmans, because he picks ticks off pigs! This pretty bird has considerably advanced in shaking off heron traditions—or sunk, as the rest of the family may possibly say. Not only does he live on ticks and grasshoppers instead of fish, but he walks about a lot, and is sociable all the time, though this is probably only accidental, and due to the fact that several find one beast convenient both as a preserve and a beater for game. Similarly one may see on the maidan tanks several Paddy-birds standing about casually on the weeds and mud, but nothing is more obvious than that they have not been introduced, and are not on speaking terms. The Buff-backed Egret is not a Calcutta bird, but some other of the Paddy-bird's relations are. I have seen the little Cinnamon Bittern (*Ardetta cinnamomea*) wild in the Zoo, and it has bred in the Botanic Gardens; and the Blue Bittern (*Dupetor flavicollis*), which is dark slate with a buff neck, bred wild in the Zoo, a year or two ago, and probably does still. Then, of course, all habitués of that exhibition know that the Night-Heron (*Nycticorax griseus*) has for years invaded the Alipore Gardens and used the islands in the middle of the tank for a combination of dormitory and nursery, in large numbers too.

So numerous, indeed, did they become, that they had to be given notice to quit, so that the heronry is now a thing of the past. The Night-Heron is much bigger than the Paddy-bird, being larger than a crow, and is unusually short-necked and thickset for a heron. The old one is slate-grey and black, while the young are brown with white spots, and look altogether different. Whether the habit of going out at night is of great benefit to this bird is hard to say, but he certainly has a very wide range being found over most of the world. The Paddy-bird is purely Indian and Burmese, and is so very common that he is one of the characteristic birds of the country. In Burma and the Andamans, however, he meets a slightly larger relative, who wears the same winter dress, but in summer plumage has a maroon ruff and slate back. This bird has been unkindly named *Ardeola bacchus*; but I am not aware that its behaviour justifies the appellation, although another member of the heron family, the Malay Bittern (*Gorsachius melanolophus*), was once captured in Ceylon in a disgraceful state of intoxication owing to indulgence in toddy.
